The Qajar Painting Collection at Leiden University Libraries

THE QAJAR PAINTING COLLECTION AT LEIDEN UNIVERSITY LIBRARIES

The Bazaar's Splendour

Forough Sajadi

LEIDEN UNIVERSITY PRESS

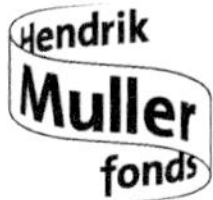 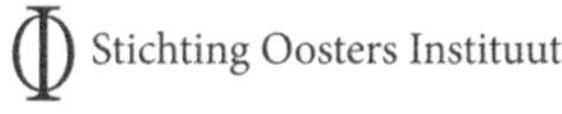 Stichting Oosters Instituut

Cover design: Andre Klijsen
Cover illustration: Wedding ceremony or execution of marriage contract, the Hotz painting collection (Or. 27 133 (2): 2).
Lay-out: Crius Group, Hulshout
Printer: Printforce B.V., Culemborg

ISBN 9789087285074
e-ISBN 9789400605718 (e-PDF)
https://doi.org/10.24415/9789087285074
NUR 644

Contact EU General Product Safety Regulation (GPSR): productsafety@lup.nl

Contents

Acknowledgements

I would like to express my gratitude to the Scaliger Institute for awarding me a fellowship at the Special Collections of Leiden University Libraries in 2023, which supported the research that led to the compilation of this catalogue. I owe a great debt of gratitude to Dr Arnoud Vrolijk, who throughout this research, supported me with his comments and valuable input. I also gratefully acknowledge the Stichting Oosters Instituut and the Dr. Hendrik Muller's Vaderlandsch Fonds Foundation for their generous contribution towards the publication costs of this book.

Introduction

The Special Collections of the Leiden University Libraries (henceforth: the UBL) house a spectacular collection from Albertus Paulus Hermanus Hotz (1855-1930), a Dutch businessman who traded with Persia intermittently between 1874 and 1903 via his company, the Persian Trading Company J.C.P. Hotz & Son (*Perzische Handels Vereeniging J.C.P. Hotz & Zoon*).[1]

Albert Hotz was born on 22 January 1855 in Rotterdam. He was the son of Jacques Cornelis Paulus Hotz (1834-1875) and Geertruida Arnolda Johanna Pino Post (1834-1912). Albert belonged to the wealthy families of Rotterdam. His father, magnate and entrepreneur, Jacques Cornelis Paulus, was the director of an iron foundry (*De Prins van Oranje*) owned by the Prince of Orange, a post from which he resigned on 1 January 1870. He then founded his own iron company, Hotz & Co, which became a major supplier to the Dutch navy and railway company.

In the 1860s, business relations between the Netherlands and Persia took a new turn. In February 1868, the Dutch government appointed Richard Charles Keun (1838-1906) as consul in Bandar Bushihr—a southwestern Persian port at the terminus of the Persian Gulf—to safeguard Dutch commercial interests and foster trade relations with Persia. Throughout Keun's efforts, a solid partnership was established among key figures and institutions, including Prince Hendrik of the Netherlands (1820-1879), Jacques Cornelis Hotz, Richard Charles Keun, Dutch Trading Company (*Nederlandsche Handels Maatschappij*), the Rotterdam Trading Association (*Rotterdamsche Handelsvereniging*), the Rotterdam Bank of Rensburg, and van Witsen. In this partnership, Hotz served as the managing partner. In October 1874, Hotz founded the Persian Trading Company J.C.P. Hotz & Son in Rotterdam. That same year, he sent his son, Albert, to Persia to open the company's office and organise its business operations there (Fig. 1).

Albert's father passed away after a short illness on 29 May 1875. Albert, who was just 20 years old, soon took over all his father's trading activities, including his business with Persia.[2] On 2 August 1875, the Hotz Company chartered a ship that set sail from Rotterdam—marking the first direct voyage from the Netherlands to Persia.[3] From that point on, Albert Hotz remained involved in business with Persia until 1903. Over the course of nearly three decades of trade, Albert Hotz amassed an extensive collection of Persian art, literature, and archival documents. Part of his collection was donated to the Leiden University Library in 1935 by Lucy Helen Woods, Hotz's widow, followed by a second donation in 1994 by Charles Albert Haccius, a grandson of Albert Hotz.[4] The 1994 donation comprises an extensive

Vertrouwelijk.-

 Ging voor de eerste keer naar Perzië in 1874 en opende kantoren

voor de door mijn vader als Gereerend vennoot, opgerichte "Perzische

Handelsvereeniging J.c.p. Hotz en Zoon" waaraan deelnamen:

    wijlen Prins Hendrik,

     de Nederlandsche Handelsmaatschappij,

     de Nederl. Consul te Buchir de heer R.C.Keun,

en de thans verdwenen Rotterdamsche Handelsvereeniging en de Com-

-manditaire Bank Rensburg en van Witsen.

 Bleef er tot Mei 1881, gedurende welke jaren ik twee keeren

eenigen tijd in Nederland doorbracht. Was sedert in Perzië in 1890/91,

1892/93 en in 1898. Mijne reizen in 1890 en 1892 geschiedden in op-

-dracht van de Imperial Bank of Persia ter behandeling van zaken met

het Perzische Gouvernement betreffende leening en den aanleg van

wegen. Hierdoor en om andere redenen kwam ik in voortdurende aanraking

met de Ministers te Teheran en de Gouverneurs der Provincien en bleef

met hen en de vertegenwoordigers van Perzië in Europa steeds op ver-

-trouwelijken voet.

 Maakte herhaaldelijk lange reizen door Perzië in nagenoeg

alle richtingen en heb mij steeds veel bezig gehouden met studie over

de literatuur van dat land, waarover ik artikels schreef in tijdschrif-

-ten (Aardrijkskundig Genootsch., Economist, Society of Arts, enz.)

 Was verschillende keeren in Rusland en besprak met den

Minister van Financien Witte en den Gouverneur van de Staatsbank, aan

wie de Russische Gezant te Teheran mij aanbevelingsbrieven had mee-

-gegeven, de beste wijze om, door bemiddeling mijner firma's, de Rus-

-sische handel in Perzie te ontwikkelen. Dit leidde tot de ondertee-

Figure 1. The first page of a letter written by Albert Hotz, in October 1904, outlining his career in Persia. The letter is preserved in the archives of the Ministry of Foreign Affairs (catalogue reference. 2.05.38), B-149, no. 1381, © The National Archives of Netherlands, the Hague.

collection of watercolour paintings, which form the focus of this contribution. The images of these paintings were published in their entirety in 2013, but the collection has never been thoroughly studied or catalogued.[5] The present catalogue aims to fill this gap.

The Hotz painting collection contains eleven sets of 247 Persian watercolours and one set of nineteen Chinese pith paintings.[6] The Persian artworks are gouaches/watercolours on richly coloured paper dating from the mid-1870s to the early 1880s, a significant proportion of which were probably made in Tehran. The artworks vary in size. Some folios have watermarks and others have embossed stamps. The subjects of the paintings vary widely, from scenes of everyday life to ceremonies, entertainment, professions, or flora and fauna, as well as a few scenes from the *Shahnama*. These paintings offer a panorama of Persian life in the Qajar period, depicting musical instruments, dance, eating habits, the legal system, medicine, customs, and fashion—especially women's clothing, and beauty conventions and accessories.

During the Qajar period, relations between Persia and the West were expanded. In particular, the fourth Qajar king, Nasir al-Din Shah (r. 1848-1896), made three official visits to Europe in 1873, 1878, and 1889. Likewise, in the nineteenth century, Westerners flocked to Persia for a variety of reasons. Throughout their stays, they were fascinated by Persian art. In response to this intense interest, a flourishing art market developed, the Hotz case being an example par excellence.[7]

The International Exhibition, Amsterdam 1883

From 1 May to 1 October 1883, the city of Amsterdam hosted the International Exhibition of Colonial and General Exports. There, Albert Hotz acted as commissioner on behalf of the Persian government (*Directeur de la Société de Commerce Persane à Rotterdam, Commissaire*). According to the general catalogue of this exhibition, in the Persian section, a broad spectrum of objects were displayed by various companies, such as the Persian Trading Company J.C.P. Hotz & Son, M. Ph. Ziegler & Co. of Manchester, and Asher, A. & Co. of Berlin, as well as a few individuals such as Amin al-Dawla (1844-1904), the Minister of Posts, and Jahangir Khan (1833/1834-1891), the Minister of Arts and Crafts (*arts et métiers*) from Tehran (Fig. 2).[8]

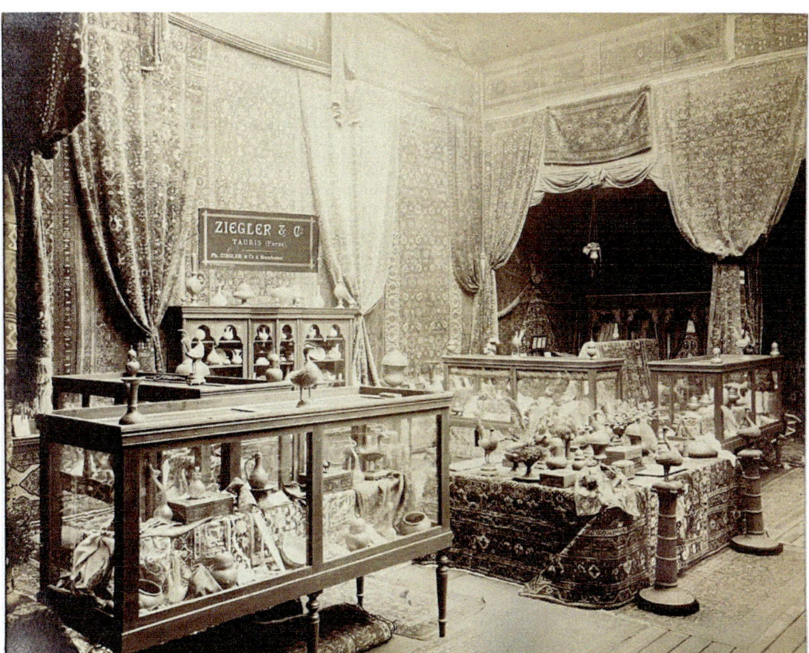

Figure 2. A photo from the Persian section of the Colonial Exhibition of Amsterdam, 1883, preserved in the UBL Hotz Album 19 (no. 19008), © Leiden University Libraries. This album contains an additional five images from the Persian section of the exhibition.

For this exhibition, alongside the general catalogue, the Hotz company published an exclusive catalogue of its objects. This catalogue was written by Jakob Eduard Polak (1818-1891), the personal physician of Nasir al-Din Shah from 1855-1860, with an emphasis on Persia from a commercial point of view (*précédé d'une Notice sur la Perse au point de vue commercial*). This catalogue provides us with descriptions of a wide range of Persian objects, especially various paintings, as seen below:

> Two paintings on canvas, representing two Persian women; one beating a drum and the other playing castanets.
>
> Seven paintings on papier-mâché, varnished, depicting the harvest, preparation and transport of opium.
>
> Two paintings on papier-mâché, varnished, depicting the hero Rostam fighting demons; relief painting.
>
> Painting depicting ancient kings of Persia, figures in relief.
>
> Painting depicting a Persian wedding.
>
> Painting depicting the Israelites crossing the Red Sea.
>
> Two paintings with flowers, birds, and Persian inscriptions. This type is used for book bindings.
>
> Various small watercolours, painted by Mirza Motalleb Khan, an excellent modern Persian artist. They depict scenes from public life, and types of the different classes of people.
>
> Painted wooden box, containing hairdressing utensils. Large papier-mâché feather boxes, decorated with paintings.
>
> Various small papier-mâché pen boxes, with Persian inscriptions, decorated with portraits, landscapes, flowers, etc.[9]

Among these artworks, one particular set attracted notable attention. In the news item, "Persia at the Exhibition", a Dutch newspaper wrote in August 1883:

> *.... a number of coloured sketches, which vividly represent the various types, crafts and services of the people. Among them are some that bear the mark of more practice and talent than is usually the case with the visual arts in Mohammedan countries.*[10]

Another Dutch newspaper pointed out these paintings as follows:

> *... an album, which is available for everyone to peruse, contains well-coloured sketches and types from Persian folk life, through which one can learn more about the various professions and businesses.*[11]

The descriptions of these artworks match the themes of numerous existing paintings at the UBL: the small-sized paintings, depicting scenes from occupations, entertainments, and various single figures. I therefore speculate that in 1883, Hotz brought part of what is now the UBL collection to the Netherlands, to be sold at the Amsterdam Exhibition.

The Artists of the UBL Collection

The Persian paintings of the Hotz collection at the UBL include 247 items. A large part of this substantial collection must have been created in the prolific workshops for the Western market. With the exception of the last set, which is poorly executed (nos. 231-247), the others are finely rendered with elaborate detail. Nonetheless, in numerous cases, the sketches and corrections are visible and the figure drawing is imperfect. Several paintings are reproduced from the originals, while the copies are made on different types of paper, with and without watermarks. The repetition of watermarks throughout this collection supports the hypothesis that a large number of the artworks were produced in a single prolific workshop (see appendix).

Notably, in Set I, 21 of the paintings carry the same watermark dated 1875, whereas seven paintings in Set II appear to bear the same watermark dated 1874. Moreover, according to the catalogue of the Amsterdam exhibition, part of the collection was in the Netherlands in 1883. This evidence pinpoints the date of the artworks to sometime from the mid-1870s to the early 1880s. In 1897, a photo of some of the paintings was published in the English book, *The Adventures of Hajji Baba of Ispahan*, where they are described as 'the collection of A. Hotz, Esq'.[12]

As discussed by Irina Dzucova in her 2022 book, three paintings from the collection, nos. 183, 186, 187, are attributed to the well-known Armenian painter, Akop Ovnatanjan (1806-1881), who worked for Nasir al-Din Shah starting in the 1860s until 1881.[13] Furthermore, the 1883 catalogue of Hotz's company reveals the identity of the artist of the paintings depicting the scenes from public life and the different classes of the people as:

Mirza Motalleb Khan, an excellent modern Persian artist.

Despite the complimentary tone of the catalogue, this painter is rather obscure among art historians of Qajar art.[14] Nevertheless, close scrutiny of the Qajar literature does yield a few Qajar records mentioning an artist named Mirza ʿAbd al-Muttalib or Mirza Muttalib.

For example, the name, Mirza Muttalib, comes up in the diary of eminent Qajar architect, Mumtahin al-Dawla (1843-1921),[15] who mentions "the late Mirza Muttalib, the painter who Haji Mirza ʿAli Khan Amin al-Dawla [the minister of the postal system] later appointed as the counsellor of the postal system (*mustashar-i postkhana, مستشار پستخانه*)".[16] Moreover, in 1877 (1294 AH), Mumtahin al-Dawla states that he has been at the house of "Mirza Shaykh Ali and Mirza Muttalib, who

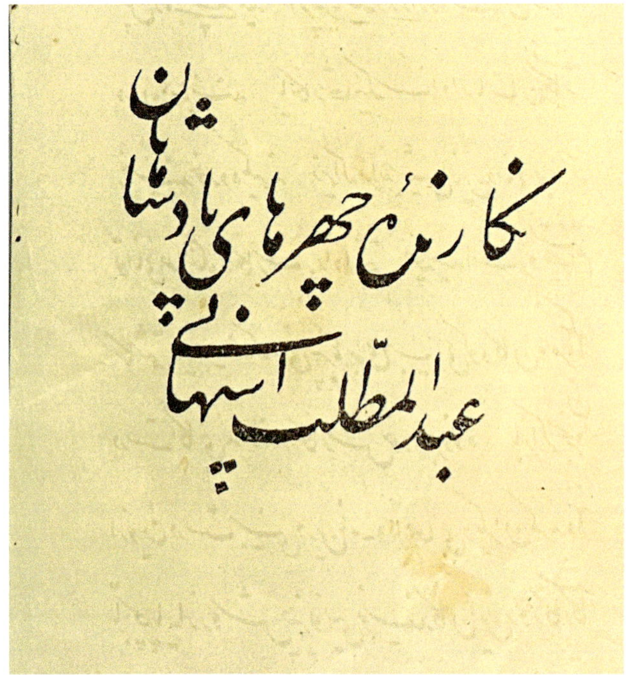

Figure 3. 'Painter of the Portraits of the Kings: 'Abd al-Muttalib Ispahani', the last page of the book of *Nama-i Khusrawan* (Tehran: 1868/1285 AH). The book is available in the UBL collection (shelf number 894 G 5).

both served the prince Jalal al-Din Mirza Qajar (1827-1872) in the preparation of the book *Nama-i Khusrawan*". He then mentions once again that this Mirza Muttalib was later appointed counsellor of the postal system.[17] This important clue led me to review the lithographed book of *Nama-i Khusrawan*, whose full title is *Nama-i Khusrawan: Dastan-i Padishahan-i Iran az Aghaz Abadiyan ta Saranjam-i Sasaniyan*, published in Tehran in 1868 (1285 AH).[18] The book included fifty-one folios depicting the ancient kings of Persia. The appendix of the book contains the credit, "Painter of the Portraits of the Kings: 'Abd al-Muttalib Ispahani" (Fig. 3). These images became a favourite pictorial convention throughout the Qajar period and were ubiquitous in various media.[19] Strikingly, the Hotz collection at the UBL includes two series after images of *Nama-i Khusrawan*, i.e., (1-41) and (42-81), which are the only known watercolour reproductions of them. I assume that these paintings were made by Mirza Muttalib's workshop at the request of Hotz's company for sale on the Western art market. Hotz knew Amin al-Dawla, the Minister of Posts, as the latter was one of the contributors to the Amsterdam Exhibition of 1883, and Mirza Muttalib was working there as a counsellor at the time (Fig. 4).[20]

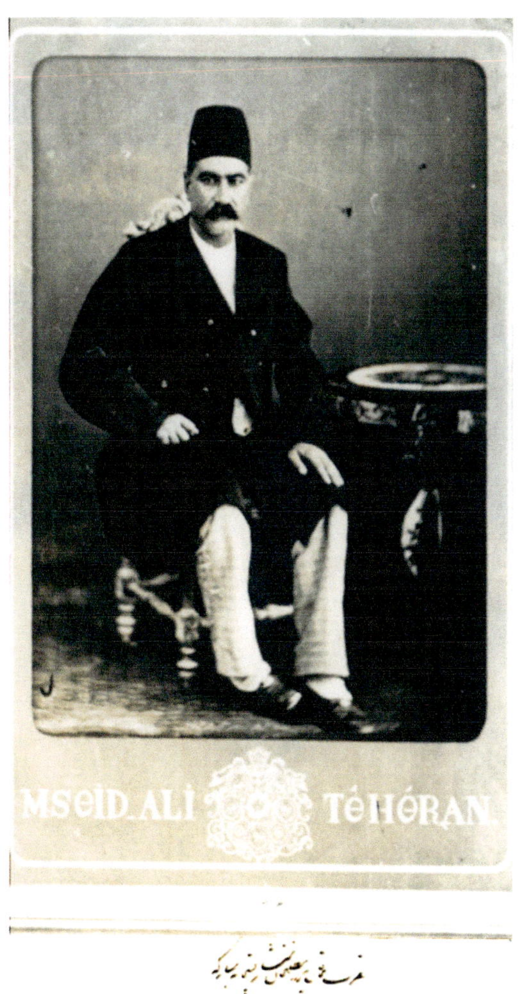

Figure 4. A photo bearing a Persian annotation that reads: 'Muqarrab al-khaqan, Mirza 'Abd al-Muttalib, the counsellor of the postal system' (مقرب الخاقان میرزا عبدالمطلب خان مستشار پستخانه مبارکه), undated, preserved at the National Library and Archives of Iran (no. 999/25/5643/3), © National Library and Archives of Iran, Tehran.

The second source is the book *Tarikh-i Muntazim-i Nasiri*, written by the distinguished Qajar statesman, I'timad al-Saltana (1843-1896). The report on the years 1881 to 1883 contains a list of the staff at the post office in the capital city (*dar al-khilafa*), Tehran, with an entry for "Mirza Muttalib, the painter (*naqqash bashi*) and the treasurer (*tahwildar*) of all post offices".[21]

Yet another important reference is a text written by Dust 'Ali Khan Mu'ayyir al-Mamalik (1876-1966). This eminent Qajar nobleman, who was himself a painter, documented his archives and memories of the Qajar family members, nobles, and artists in a series of papers. In one of his texts, there is an entry about Mirza 'Abd al-Muttalib Mustashar ("Counsellor"), saying that he was one of the students sent by Nasir al-Din Shah to study in Europe. Later, his daughter, Khujasta Khanum, became the last wife of Nasir al-Din Shah. This source also reiterates that Amin al-Dawla appointed this painter as a counsellor in the postal system, and that he was henceforth known as Mustashar. The text points out that Mirza ʿAbd al-Muttalib was a master watercolour painter, and includes a photograph of him.[22] Among his works, there is a fine painting of Muzaffar al-Din Shah (r. 1896-1907), dated 1896 (1314 AH), and signed as "painted by the most humble, ʿAbd al-Muttalib" (*raqam-i kamtarin al-ʿAbd Muttalib*), preserved at Gulistan Palace, Tehran.[23]

An Overview of the Collection: Sets I-XI (Or. 27.133 (2): 1-247)

Before going through the catalogue, a brief overview of the collection is in order. The paintings are categorised in 11 sets. The inventory numbers are based on the existing records at the UBL, where they are written in pencil on the back of the folios. Five folios carry a pencil note in the lower right margin beginning with T: no. 213 (probably T2), no. 206 (T5), no. 231 (T7), no. 40 (T9), and no. 238 (T10). It is unclear who wrote these notes and what they mean. In addition, some folios bear Persian numbers and notes, which will be explained.

Set I: Or. 27.133 (2): 1-41

The set consists of twenty folded double leaves and one single folio (no. 41). The paintings are embedded in a decorative frame approximately 7-9 mm in length and several rulings in blue, greyish, and golden tones. The physical appearance of the bi-folios suggests that the set was intended to be an album, with a section on everyday life followed by a section on ancient figures.

All folios have watermarks and exhibit pronounced laid lines.[24] The watermarks are as follows: (1) A shield with three crescents and a fleur-de-lis. The top of the shield is decorated with a bust of a donkey. A banner on the shield bears the inscription 'LESCHALLAS' and the date of 1875 appears below the shield. (2) The joined sheet contains a countermark with a circle decorated with an imperial crown and the inscription 'PRO BONO PUBLICO'. The inscription 'UNIVERSAL FOOLSCAP' appears underneath the banner.[25]

The rectos depict the twenty ancient kings of Persia, copied from the known Qajar lithographed *Nama-i Khusrawan* (Fig. 5). The joined pages (verso folios) include twenty genre paintings. The garments of the figures and the backdrops suggest that the paintings display the socio-cultural life of the middle class in the Qajar period. Of these, twelve paintings represent an extensive account of everyday life. It begins with the depiction of marriage morals (nos. 2, 4, 6, 8, 10, 12, 26, 32), which was an immensely popular theme in the Qajar period and is abundantly represented as single works and as a series.[26]

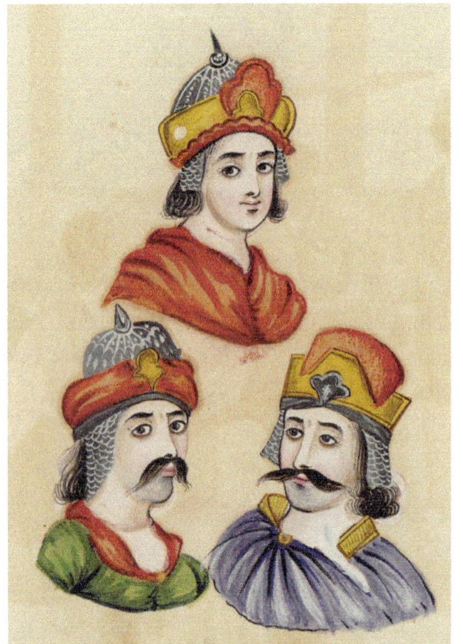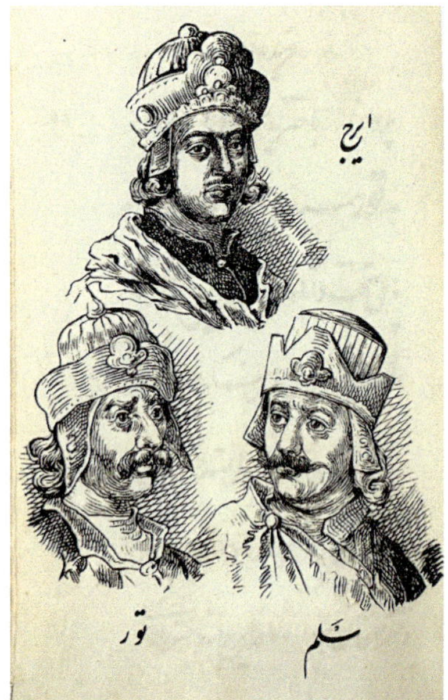

Figure 5. Left: The painting from the Hotz painting collection (no. 23). Right: Lithograph from *Nama-i Khusrawan*, published in Tehran in 1868. The image is reproduced after a copy preserved in the UBL collection (Shelf Number 894 G 5), page 94.

This is followed by intimate scenes of the newlyweds at home (nos. 14, 16, 18), then the episode of childbirth, the boy's circumcision, and a scene of his schooling (nos. 22, 36, 40). Of these scenes, intimacy and school are long-established themes in Persian painting, while this circumcision scene is one of but a few examples throughout the Persian painting tradition.[27]

This set also includes a story about a love affair (nos. 20, 24, 38). Although in folio no. 38, the hands and toes are clumsily rendered, the painter has depicted the crucial details: the culprit, barefoot and head shaven, is being led by a string through his nose, which is bleeding profusely (Fig. 6).[28]

Yet, there are two paintings, no. 30 and no. 34, which illustrate the theme of entertainment. No. 30 shows a nighttime street performance and audience.[29] No. 34 depicts entertainers rehearsing. In the background, a middle-aged man in a turban is leading another man by a halter. Based on the annotation of another Qajar painting sold by Bonhams in 2022, this man is identified as Mulla Nasruddin, a prominent figure in Persian and Middle Eastern folklore.[30] These two paintings capture a scene from the story *Stealing the Mulla's Donkey* (Fig. 7).[31]

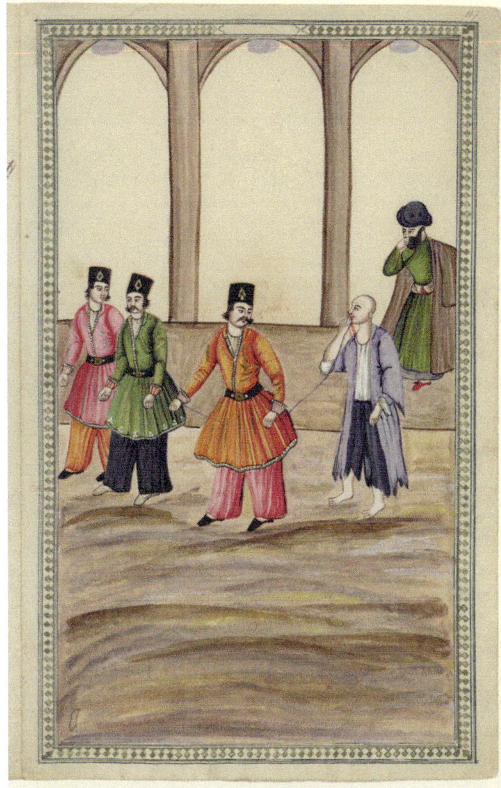

Figure 6. 'A culprit with a string through his nose, led through the bazaar', the Hotz painting collection (no. 38).

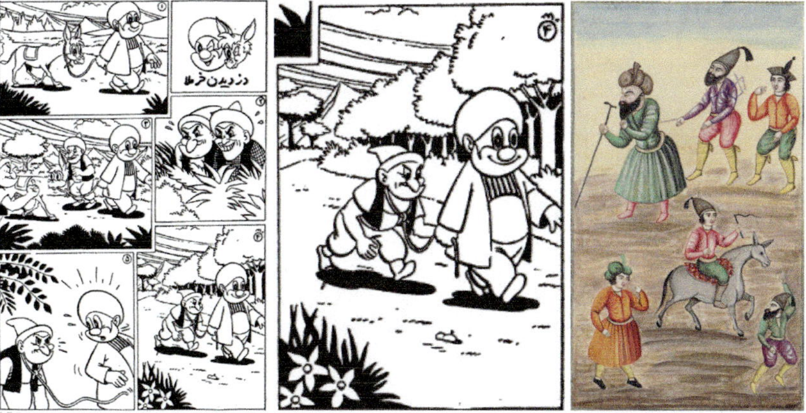

Figure 7. Left: The cartoon of *Stealing the Mulla's Donkey*, published in *Tawfiq Book: Mulla Nasruddin: the first illustrated collection of the famous jokes of 'Mulla' as the cartoon strip* (1348/1969), n.p. The book is in the author's collection. Middle: a detail of the comic strip, no. 4. Right: a painting from the Hotz collection (no. 34).

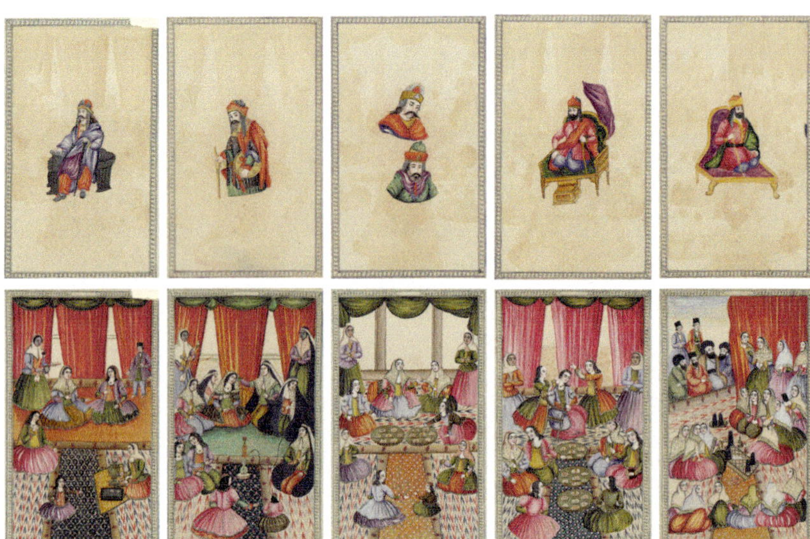

Figure 8. Above, from left to right: the recto folio, copied from the lithographed book *Nama-i Khusrawan*, published in Tehran in 1868, pages 114-33. Below: on the versos, an account of marriage customs. The folios have Persian numbers written in pencil in the upper left margin. The numbers, from left to right, are 10, 11, 12, 13, 14.

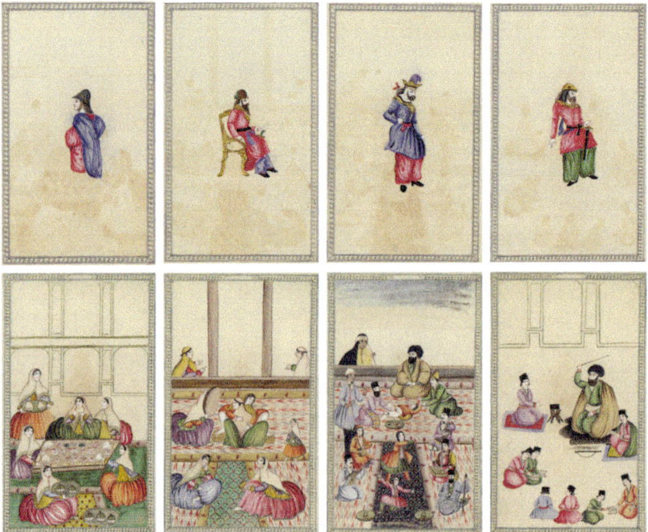

Figure 9. Above, from left to right: the recto folio, copied from the lithographed book *Nama-i Khusrawan* (1868); see pages 207-66. Below, from left to right: verso: episodes in the life of a boy: home festivity, birth, circumcision, and school. The folios have Persian numbers written in pencil in the upper left margin. The numbers, from left to right, are 22, 23, 24, 25.

It is worth noting that on all the verso folios, there are faint numbers written in Persian visible in the upper left margin. I suspect that they were intended to guide the reader through the sequence of the account. To test this hypothesis, if the paintings are aligned according to the Persian numbers, two stories are recognisable, while the corresponding rectos match up perfectly with the sequence of *Nama-i Khusrawan* (Figs. 8, 9). In other episodes, however, the numbers do not match up with *Nama-i Khusrawan*'s book sequence. Based on the fact that the recto images do not include all the images in *Nama-i Khusrawan*, I would assume that the workshop produced additional bi-folios that Hotz's company most probably put up for sale.

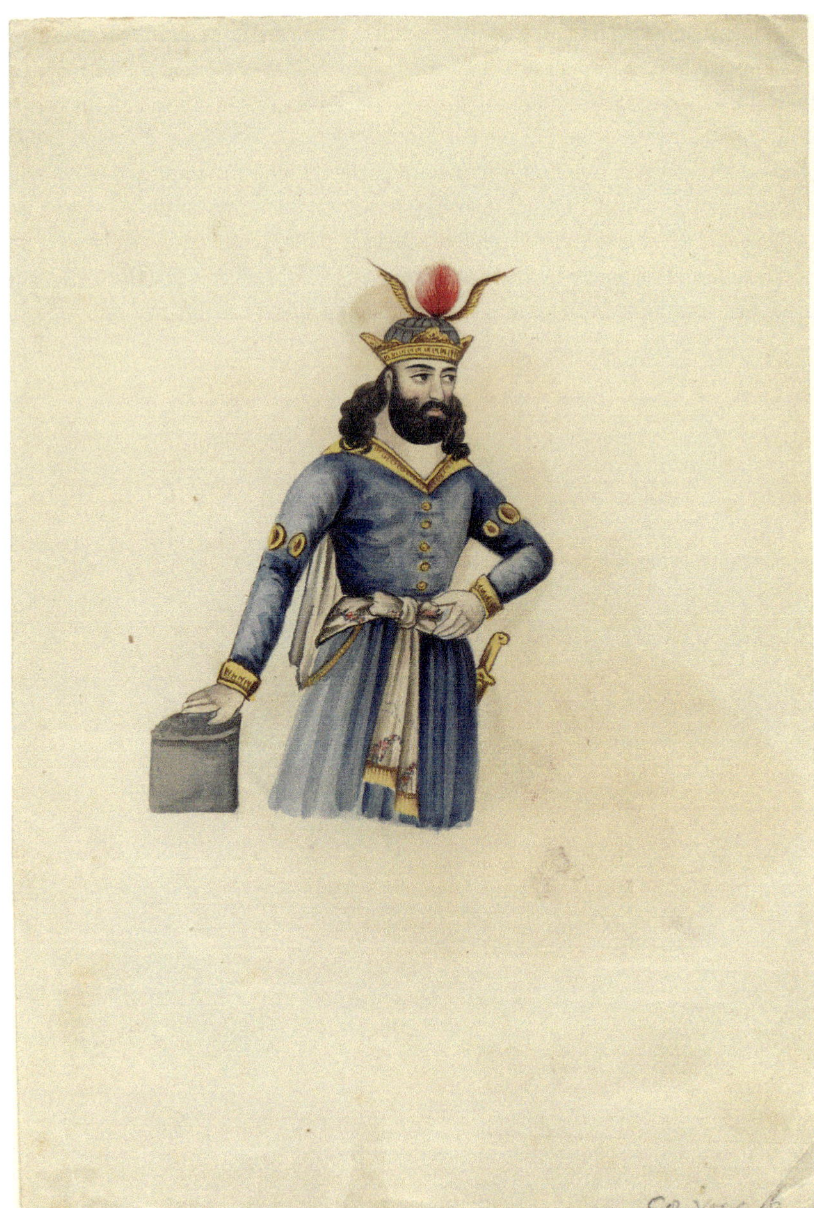

Figure 10. 'Yazdgird XV', the Hotz painting collection (no. 81v). The page bears a short Dutch note, written in pencil at the bottom right, which reads '58 voor 6' (58 for 6).

Set II: Or. 27.133 (2): 42-81

This set includes forty-one paintings, comprising thirty-nine single folios, plus one page (no. 81) with paintings on both sides. Similar to Set I (1-40), recto, the paintings in this set portray ancient personages, reproduced after the Qajar lithographic *Nama-i Khusrawan*. Nevertheless, the folios of Set II are smaller than in Set I. The paintings also have different characteristics; although neither set is of the same standard of craftsmanship, the faces in this set are fleshier.

Except folio no. 81, which has no watermark, all the folios have the same watermarks as in Set I. On the watermarks of paintings nos. 44, 45, 51, 54, 65, 71, 78, the date of 1874 is detectable. With the exception of folio 81, the thirty-nine paintings bear two short Persian annotations indicating the names of the protagonists, one finely in ink and the other crudely in pencil. Interestingly, page 81v bears a short Dutch note, written in pencil at the bottom right, which reads '58 voor 6' (58 for 6). I conjecture that this note was made by Hotz, indicating the number of works and their price, although the currency is unknown (Fig. 10).

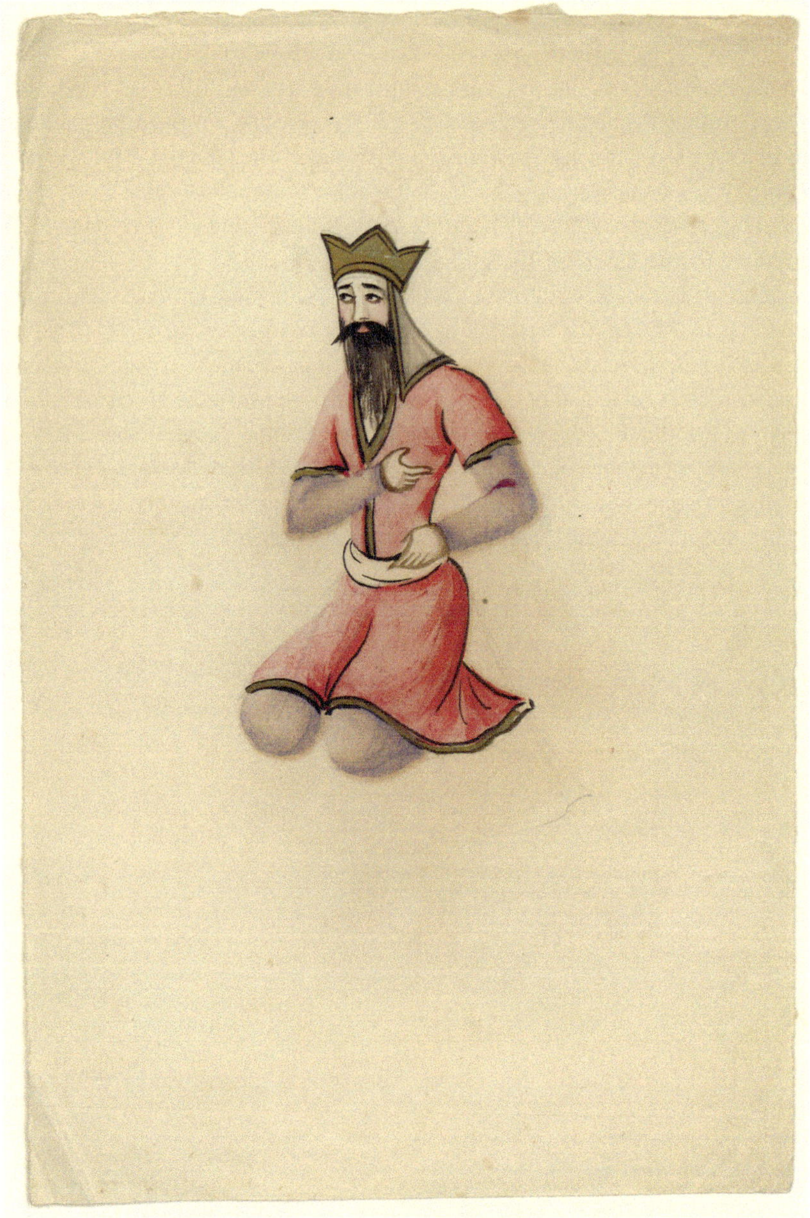

Figure 11. 'A seated man in a red robe with a beard', the Hotz painting collection (no. 89).

Set III: Or. 27.133 (2): 82-96

This set includes fifteen folios depicting single male figures dressed in contemporary administrative and governmental attire. The figures are not personalised, but have a variety of beard styles, outfits, and poses. The paintings have such similar characteristics that they must have been made from a common template. In several cases, the outlines and corrections of the sketches are visible. For example, the sketch on folio no. 89 shows that the painter changed his mind from a standing figure to the present seated man (Fig. 11).

None of the different types of paper bear a watermark. On folio no. 92, there is a faint embossed stamp at the bottom, to the left of the image. Although I have been unable to decipher the stamp, what is clear is that it is different from the embossed stamps of folios 107 and 221. These stamps are either of the owner's seal or the motto of the paper manufacturer.[32]

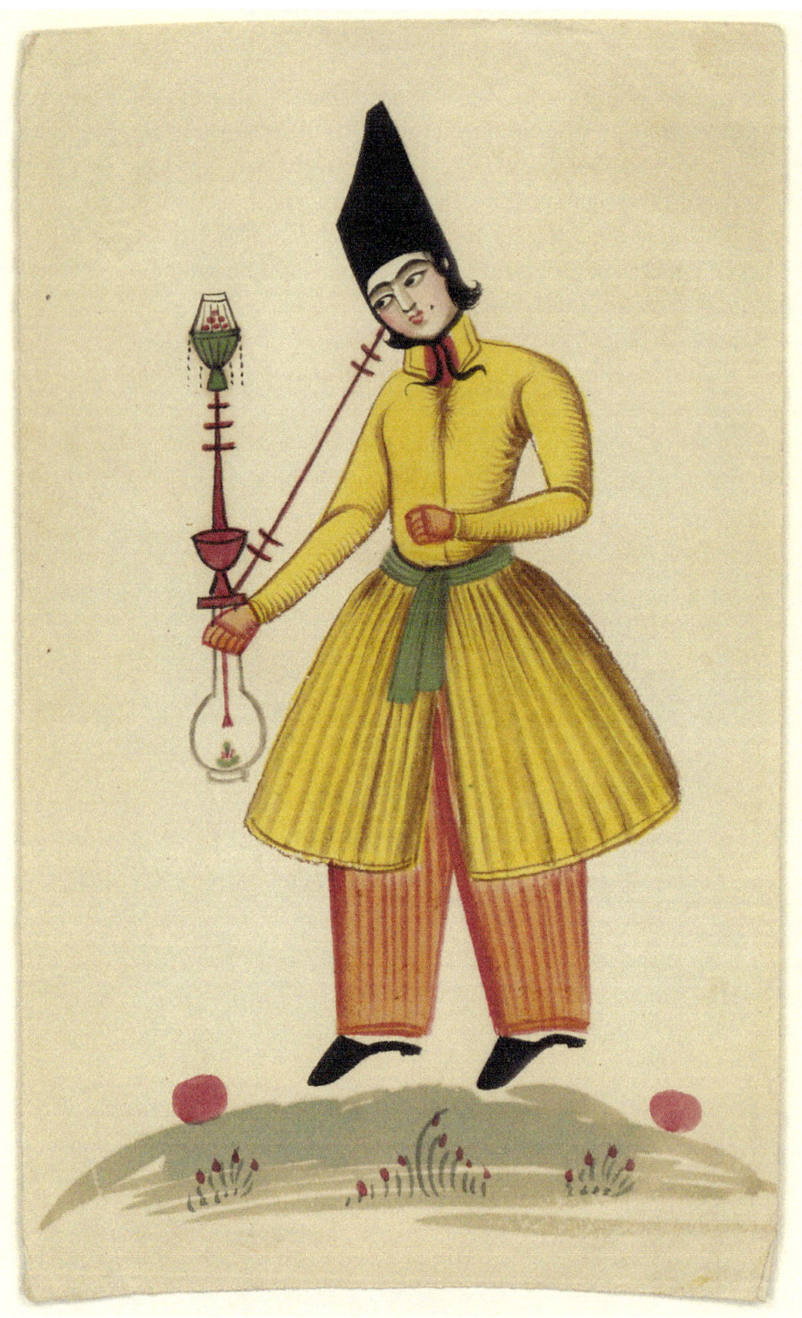

Figure 12. 'A young Qajar official holding a water pipe (*qalyan*)', the Hotz painting collection (no. 101).

Set IV: Or. 27.133 (2): 97-106

This set contains individual figures dressed in contemporary attire, nos. (97, 100), (98, 99), (101, 102, 103), (104, 105, 106). The paintings have been made from models. The figures are set on a green-brownish ground embellished with tufts of grass or flowers. Sometimes two or three red balls (probably apples) decorate the setting. These paintings must have been made in a prolific workshop. Paintings nos. 101-103 are reproductions, and yet there was another copy of this design in the possession of another Western collector (Fig. 12).[33]

The paintings are all on a single type of paper, which in all cases is roughly cut. On closer inspection, the pattern of the mould's wires is visible. Folios 97, 99, 100 bear a watermark.[34]

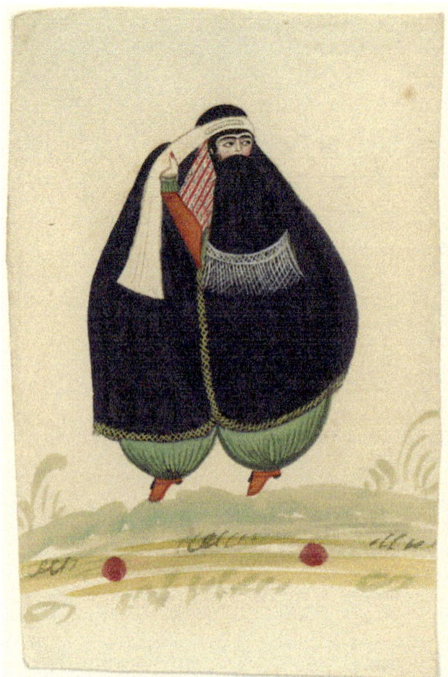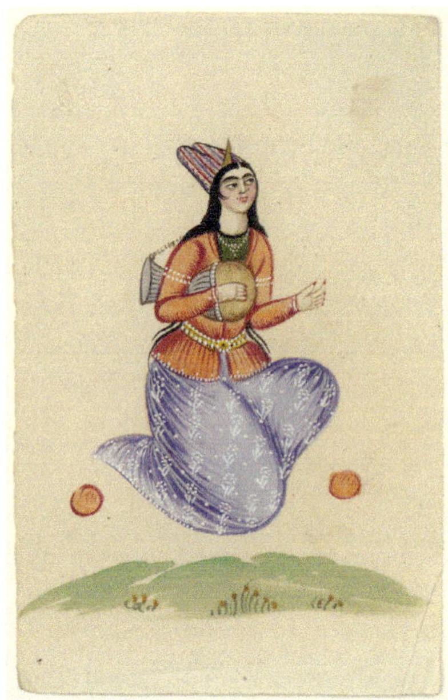

Figure 13. Two paintings from the Hotz painting collection. Left: 'A woman wearing a chador and green pantaloons' (no. 109). Right: 'A dancing girl playing the goblet drum (*tombak*)' (no. 123).

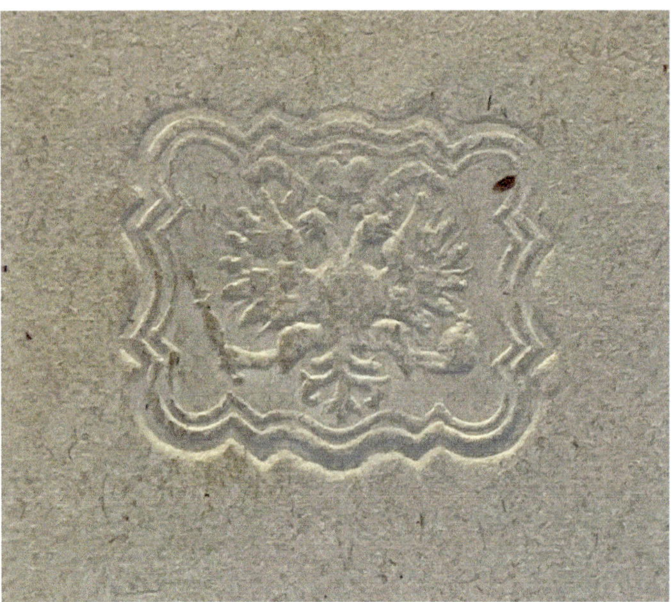

Figure 14. Detail, embossing stamp, the Hotz painting collection (no. 123).

Set V: Or. 27.133 (2): 107-142

This set includes thirty-six single figures of women,[35] shown in a variety of poses and gestures, both indoors and outdoors, some wearing a chador (veil) and some not. Twelve figures are playing instruments, five are dancing, eight are holding fans, one is holding a glass, and one is holding a mirror (Fig. 13). Interestingly, another version of painting no. 123 was in the possession of another Western collector.[36]

In the nineteenth century, Persian women garnered the attention of Westerner visitors, who described the public and private lives of Persian women intriguingly in their travelogues.[37] Accordingly, artworks depicting this subject were a favourite among Westerners. There are abundant examples of these paintings as albums and single pages, such as the several pages from the collection of Jean Pozzi (1884-1967), dated the mid-nineteenth century, in the Museum of Art and History in Geneva;[38] the five folios of an album dated c. 1850, in the British Museum (P&D 2001,0728.60);[39] and thirty-six folios in this set of the Hotz collection.

This set has certain points which merit closer attention. The paintings in this set are somewhat related to the previous sets: folios 107-123 have the same mise-en-scène as the ones in Set IV, nos. 79-109. Nevertheless, the paper exhibits different features. Folio no. 109 carries a watermark which does not occur in any other folio in the Hotz collection.[40] The female figures in folios no. 138-141 have a similar palette and dress to the male figures in this set and in Set III, nos. 82-96. These paintings were probably mass produced in the same workshop as those of Sets III and IV. Moreover, careful examination reveals that folios 124-137 were temporarily kept in a frame with a size of approx. 13×18/18.5 cm. A number of folios bear an embossed stamp, such as folio no. 107, which bears a Russian embossed stamp in the upper right corner of the image.[41]

Baines's study explains that some folios bear only part of the watermark, and that by joining the folios together, the whole watermark can be seen, e.g. folios 127 and 130: 'SMITH & MEYNIER', 'FIUME'.[42] These watermarks can be seen in folio no. 134 'FIUME' and no. 132 'SMITH & MEYNIER'. This watermark refers to the paper mill in the city of Fiume (today Rijeka, Croatia). There is also an oval watermark on folios 136 and 137.

On folio no. 123, at the top left of the image, there is a stamp with the watermark of a double-headed eagle. The eagle's claws hold a sceptre and an orb. As this symbol is the coat of arms of the Russian Empire, the paper may have been made in Russia (Fig. 14).

Furthermore, folio no. 120 has a faint trace of an oval stamp. It is at the bottom, to the right of the drummer, surrounding the apple. Folio no. 142 has a faint stamp at the bottom, on the left foot of the tambourine player. This stamp is probably the same as in Set VI, no. 144.[43]

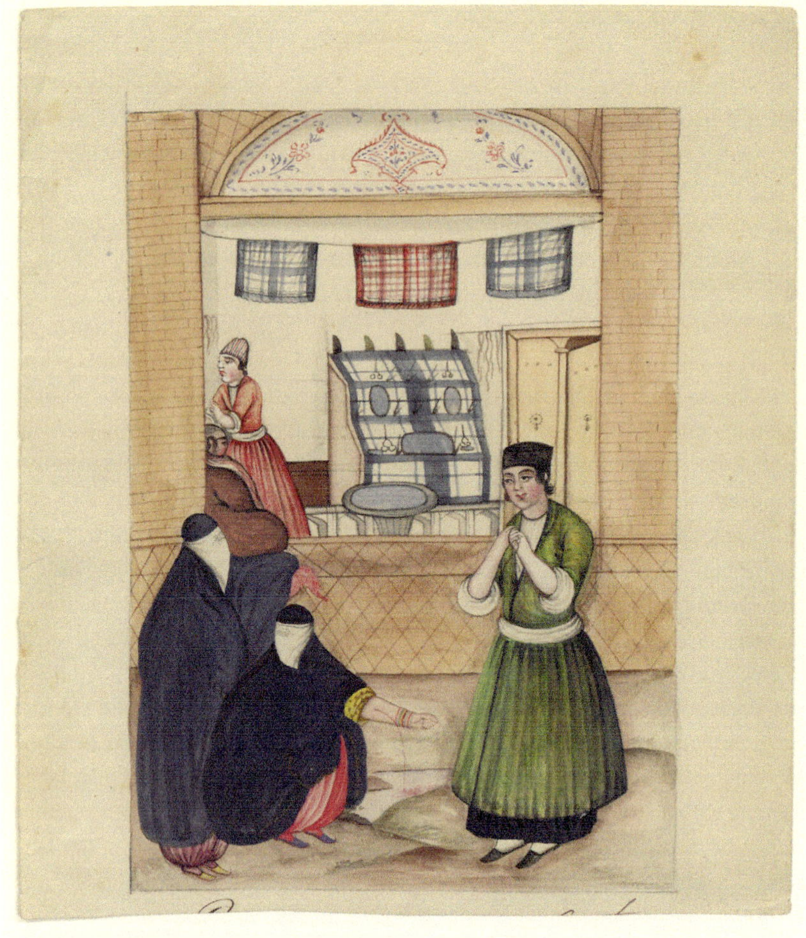

Figure 15. 'A barber performs bloodletting on a woman', the Hotz painting collection (no. 176).

Set VI: Or. 27.133 (2): 143-147, 149-150, 154, 168-182, 184

This set depicts various professions of the Qajar period in two forms: (1) 26 folios with individual figures (nos. 143-147, 149-150, 182, 184); (2) 14 folios in a bazaar setting (nos. 168-181).

The bazaar folios are cut out, but there is evidence to suggest that the papers once bore Western annotations, none of which currently exist. Meanwhile, four folios carry Persian annotations (nos. 172, 175, 179, 180).

The painters of the bazaar set employed a delicately balanced mise-en-scène throughout, depicting the local architecture and capturing the lively interaction between people and shopkeepers. The faces of the figures are finely rendered. In no. 176, a bloodletting scene, the woman patient looks away, afraid to see the blood. However, some of the preparatory sketching is still visible. In folio no. 170, for example, the painter's original idea of placing a large vase on the counter, to the right of the viewer, shows through.

Among these folios, nos. 176 and 181 stand out as rare, and perhaps unique, visual testimony of practices from this period. No. 176 contains the bloodletting scene (فصد، رگ زنی، خون گرفتن), performed by a barber (Fig. 15), while no. 181 probably depicts a marionette puppet shop (خیمه شب بازی).[44]

Since the Safavid period (1501-1722), bazaar scenes had traditionally appeared in illuminated manuscripts.[45] However, in the Qajar period, this subject matter became a theme in its own right. This popularity stemmed from the enthusiasm of Western travellers to explore domestic Persian culture and the dynamics of their marketplaces. Along these lines, Charles James Wills (died 1912), a British man who served as the physician of the Indo-European Telegraph Department in Persia from 1866 to 1881, published a book of his observations.[46] In his book, published in 1891, he describes the Isfahan bazaar and includes a picture of 'three shops in the bazaar (from a native drawing)', which perfectly matches the hand of the Hotz bazaar scenes. Later, in another book in 1897, he published several paintings of bazaar scenes from his collection (Fig. 16). The profound similarities between Will's and Hotz's paintings indicate that these artworks were produced in one prolific workshop.[47] This observation gives rise to various questions, such as whether Wills commissioned these paintings himself or bought them through Hotz's company. I will leave such speculation open for future researchers.[48]

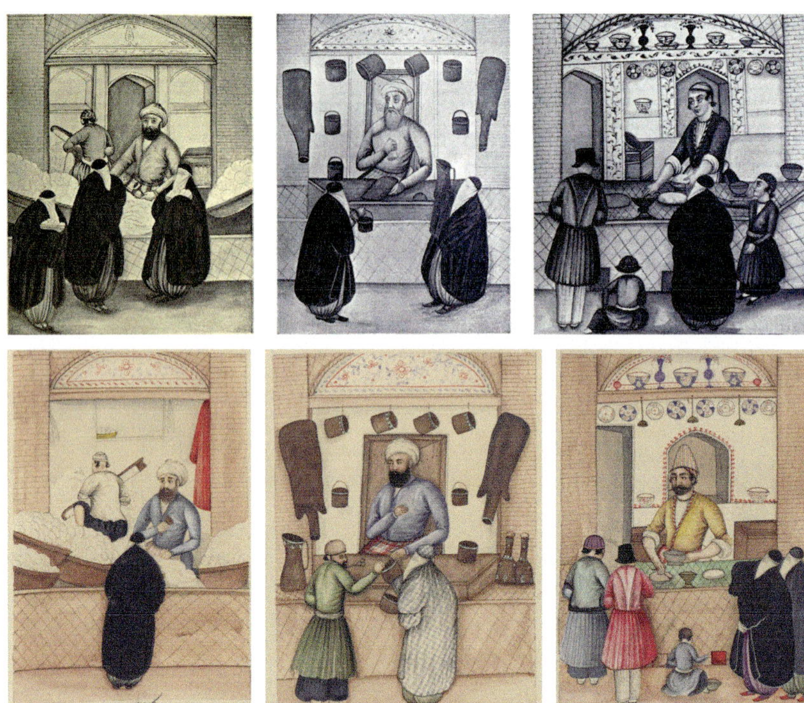

Figure 16. Above, from left to right: 'A cotton-carder', 'A leather-bucket maker', 'A seller of pilau (rice) and soup', from the collection of Dr Wills. The photos are reproduced after *The Adventures of Hajji Baba of Ispahan*, published in 1897, pages 37, 289, 357. Below, from left to the right: three corresponding paintings from the Hotz painting collection (nos. 179, 169, 170).

In the same vein, the occupations have been depicted in copious artworks with different qualities and characteristics, e.g., an album in the Museum of Islamic Art, Doha (MS.722.2011), d. second half of the nineteenth century, containing thirty-seven scenes, among them several folios depicting bazaar scenes.[49] Also, there are the twenty tiles depicting professions in the State Museums of Berlin, Ethnological Museum,[50] and several unfinished drawings in the Harvard album (1960.161, fols. 13-16), d. nineteenth century.[51]

In this set, folio no. 144 carries a Russian embossed stamp on the left, below the figure's feet. This stamp is similar to that of Set V, folio no. 142.[52] Likewise, folios 150 and 151 bear traces of this embossed stamp.

Set VII: Or. 27.133 (2): 148, 151-153, 155-167

The quality and characteristics of the paintings are consistent with some of Set V and Set VI. The paintings mainly depict individual figures engaged in a variety of activities, such as the traditional Persian gymnasium or *zurkhana* (زورخانه), swinging *mils* (Indian clubs) (میل زدن), swinging a *kabbada* (کباده زدن),[53] and flying pigeons (کفتربازی). There are also some depictions of figures playing instruments or rehearsing with objects and animals, which were mainly used for street theatre or traditional street performances (معرکه گیری). These amusements were recorded by Western visitors such as Hotz in their texts and photos (Fig. 17),[54] and were also captured visually in numerous Qajar artworks, including this set. Among similar examples from other collections, there is an enchanting long paper painting, d. 1873-1907, preserved in the National Museums of World Culture in Gothenburg (0000.00.0518c), which contains various scenes including musicians performing, as well as animal trainers and activities from the *zurkhana*.[55]

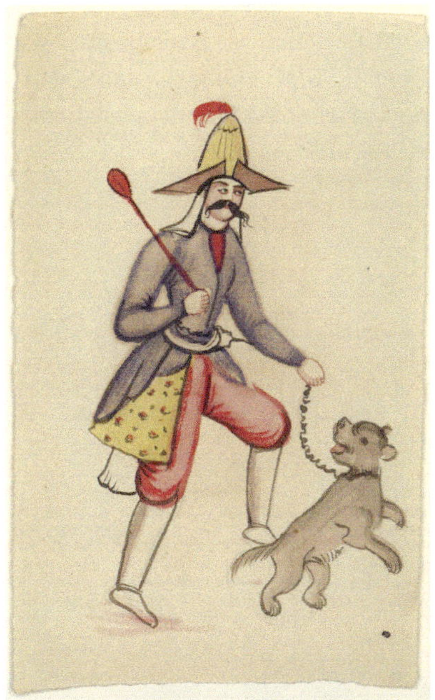
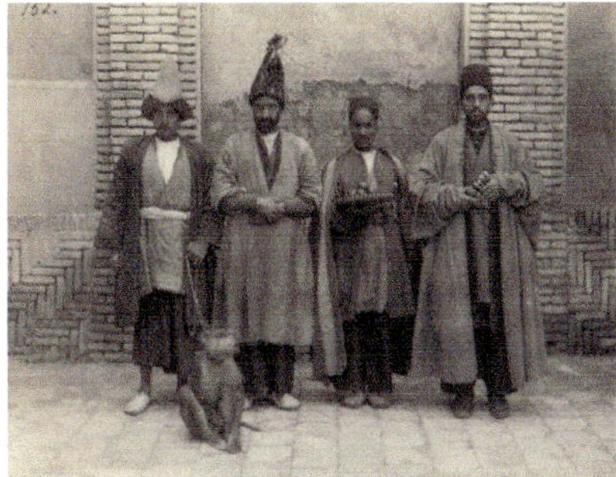

Figure 17. Left: 'An entertainer with a yellow cap rehearsing with a dog', Hotz painting collection (no. 165). Right: 'Portrait of a group of *lutis* (jesters) with a monkey in Sultanabad (present-day Arak)', d. 1890-1891. The photo was taken by A. Hotz, the Wereldmuseum Rotterdam (TM-FV-1213-86). © Wereldmuseum Rotterdam.

In this set, some technical aspects deserve attention. Nos. 166 and 167 are on a different type of paper than the rest of the set. Similarly to Set V, folios 124-137, they were briefly kept in a frame with a size of c. 13×18/18.5 cm. Folio no. 166 bears the watermark 'FIUME' (as with folios 127, 134), and folio 167 bears the watermarks 'SMITH & MEYNIER' (similar to folios 130, 132), indicating the paper mill in Fiume (present-day Rijeka, Croatia).

Set VIII: Or. 27.133 (2): 183, 185-187, 199, 203-207

These paintings portray various individual figures. Folios 183, 186, 187 are executed in a masterful hand. All three are on the same type of thick paper, which is not used in any of the other folios in the Hotz collection. Of these three, no. 186, depicting a mulla (ملا), bears a striking resemblance to a painting in the collection of Jean-Baptiste Feuvrier (died 1926), Nasir al-Din Shah's personal physician from 1889 to 1892 (Fig. 18).

In 2022, Irina Dzucova attributed these three paintings from Hotz's collection to Akop Ovnatanjan (1806-1881).[56] Ovnatanjan was the Armenian painter, who was in Persia from the 1860s until 1881. In Persia, he was in Tabriz and then in the capital, Tehran. Ovnatanjan created copious artworks, including watercolour paintings, "intended for the Shah and for sale to foreigners".[57] Nasir al-Din Shah named him 'naqqash bashi' (head of the court painters) and awarded him the medal of the Order of Science (نشان علمی) for his merits and achievements.[58]

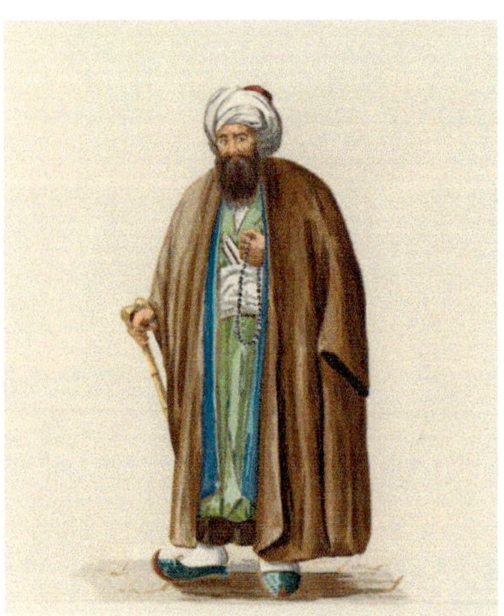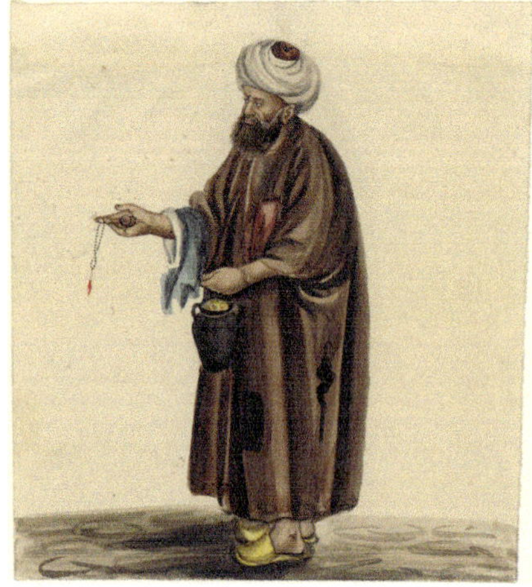

Figure 18. Left: 'Mulla Ismail, performing Istikhara, from a watercolour album of Dr Feuvrier, reproduction from the book *Trois ans à la cour de Perse*, by Jean-Baptiste Feuvrier, d. 1900, 321. This image was copied in *Du Khorassan au pays des Backhtiaris, trois mois de voyage en Perse* by D'Allemagne, Henri René, vol. 1, d. 1911, 132. Right: Hotz painting collection (no. 186).

Set IX: Or. 27.133 (2): 188-198, 200-202

These paintings all employ a cartouche, the subject matter being a mélange of indoor and outdoor scenes such as playing music, relaxing, and hunting.

Although some papers have watermarks already identified in the previous sets, folios 206 and 207 bear a different watermark from the ones that we have seen thus far. Also of note is the embossed stamp on folio 195 depicting the *Shir u Khurshid* (Lion and Sun). This symbol has a long-standing history in Persian art. In particular, in the Qajar period, it was used ubiquitously in a number of media in art, both religious and secular, and in contexts from the royal court to folk art.[59] Folio no. 203 contains a trace of an embossed stamp in the upper right-hand corner.

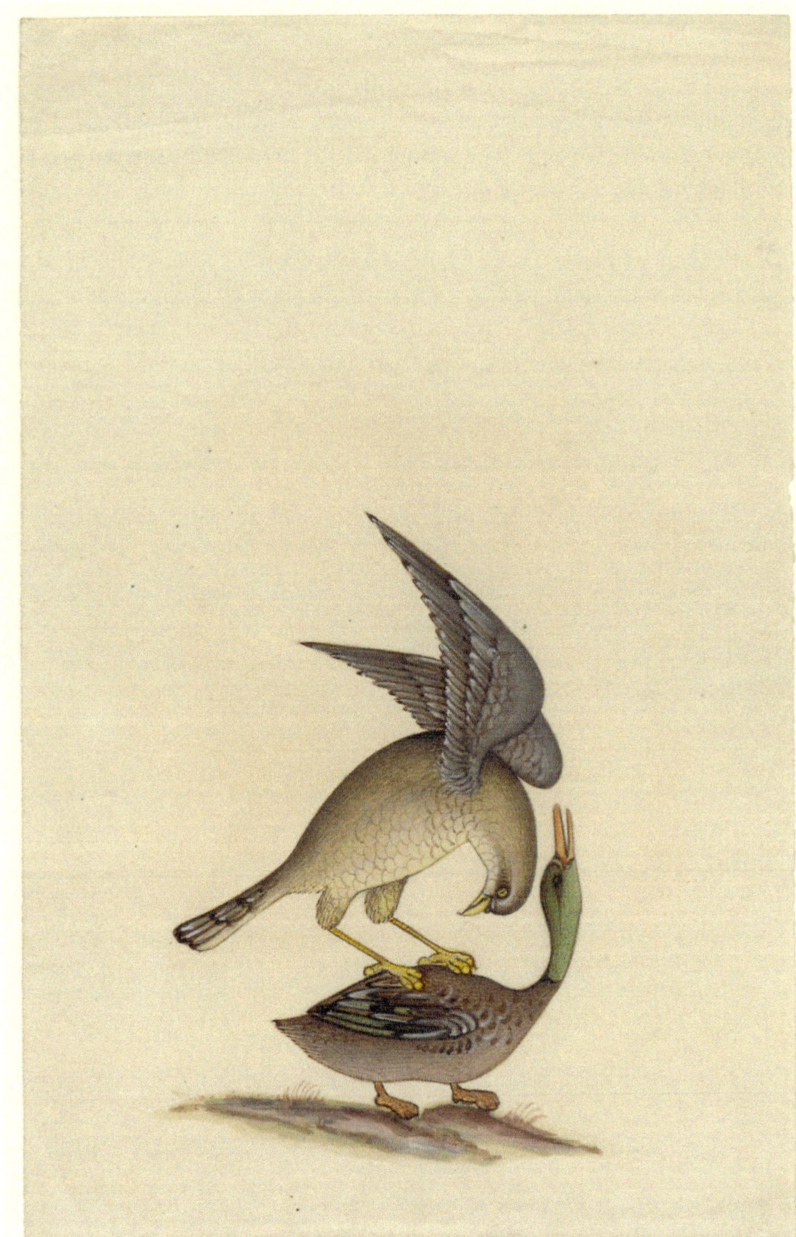

Figure 19. An eagle hunting a mallard, the Hotz painting collection (no. 212).

Set X: Or. 27.133 (2): 208-230

This set is dedicated to the theme of flora and fauna. Compositions with flowers, birds, and butterflies became increasingly popular in the Safavid period (1502-1722), and remained so through the Qajar period.[60] Some of the set's animal paintings reflect long-established pictorial conventions, such as nos. 212 and 220. For example, folio no. 212 depicts an eagle hunting a mallard, a motif which has a long history in Islamic art, dating back to the twelfth and thirteenth centuries.[61] This pictorial convention remained popular in the art of later periods, for example in the plaster decorations (گچبری) of the Borujerdi House in Kashan, dating from the Qajar period (Figure 19).[62]

Folio no. 220 depicts a camel fight, whose pictorial history dates back to the sixteenth century.[63] Nos. 218 and 219 are copies of a lion devouring the thigh of a deer. This work is comparable to the folio "A Lion Devouring the Thigh of a Deer", dated to the second half of the nineteenth century, signed Mirza Husayn, at the Museum of Art and History in Geneva (1971-0107-0358).

In addition to the popularity of flora and fauna in Persian art, it is worth mentioning that these paintings underscore Hotz's interest in Persia's wildlife. Significantly, Masaharu Yoshida (1852-1921), a Japanese diplomat in Persia in the period 1880-1881, met Hotz and noted that Hotz kept a lion at his residence in Bushihr, a port city in southwestern Persia.[64] A note also indicates that Hotz brought a *Callimenus dasypus*, a species of grasshopper, from Persia to the Netherlands and donated it to the National Museum of Natural History in Leiden in 1891.[65]

In terms of paper characteristics, this set contains different types of paper than the previous ones. Some folios have a watermark, while others do not. Among these, folio no. 224 bears a distinctive watermark.[66] Folio no. 230 has a faint embossed stamp.

Set XI: Or. 27.133 (2): 231-247

These paintings represent a variety of themes, crudely executed on low-quality paper. Notwithstanding recent conservation efforts by Juliet Baines in the period 2016-2017, they remain in a fragile condition.

In folios 235, 236, 242-244, the figures' garments and the vessel's flag refer to Ottoman art and culture. Folio no. 231 depicts the *Shir u Khurshid* (Lion and Sun), which became the national symbol in the Qajar period.[67] Folio no. 247 carries the Qur'anic maxim *Support from Allah, and imminent victory* (نصر من الله و فتح قريب), which was common in Qajar buildings, both public and private.[68]

There are also two scenes from the *Shahnama*, the Persian national epic, which has been the most decorated book in Persia throughout the centuries. This set includes the depiction of two characters from the *Shahnama*: Suhrab (no. 239) and the battle of Rostam and the White Div (demon) (no. 241).

Catalogue of Individual Items

Or. 27.133 (2): 1: Kay Kavus II.[69] Page: 20.4×32.3, frame: 30.9×18.7 cm (see no. 64).

Or. 27.133 (2): 2: Wedding ceremony or execution of marriage contract (عقد). Page: 32.2×20.4 cm, frame: 30.8×18.8 cm. The Persian numerals ۱۴ (14) are written in pencil in the upper left margin and the number 115 in Western script in the lower right margin. This folio is associated with nos. 6, 4, 10, 12.

Or. 27.133 (2): 3: Kay Gubad I. Page: 32.3×20.6, frame: 30.8×18.7 cm (see no. 66).

Or. 27.133 (2): 4: Preparation of the bride. Page: 32.3×20.5 cm, frame: 30.8×18.7 cm. The Persian numerals ۱۳ (13) are written in pencil in the upper left margin. This folio is associated with nos. 6, 10, 12, 2.

Or. 27.133 (2): 5: Nozar VIII. Page: 32.2×20.5 cm, frame. 30.9×18.8 cm.

Or. 27.133 (2): 6: Asking the groom's family to visit the bride's house. Page: 32.2×20.5 cm, frame: 30.9×18.8 cm. The Persian numerals ۱۰ (10) are written in pencil in the upper left margin. This folio is associated with nos. 4, 10, 12, 2.

Or. 27.133 (2): 7: Alexander X. Page: 32.2×20.4 cm, frame: 30.4×18.3 cm (see no. 62).

Or. 27.133 (2): 8: Women's feast. Page: 32.2×20.4 cm, frame: 30.9×18.8 cm. The Persian numerals ۲۲ (22) are written in pencil in the upper left margin. This folio is associated with nos. 22, 36, 40.

Or. 27.133 (2): 9: Zab and Garshasb. Page. 32.2×20.5 cm, frame: 30.9×18.9 cm (see no. 80).

Or. 27.133 (2): 10: Ladies engaging in festivities.[70] Page: 32.2×20.5 cm, frame: 30.9×18.7 cm. The Persian numerals ۱۲ (12) are written in pencil in the upper left margin. This folio is associated with nos. 6, 4, 12, 2.

Or. 27.133 (2): 11: Afrasiyab IX. Page: 32.3×20.4 cm, frame: 30.8×18.6 cm.

Or. 27.133 (2): 12: Marriage proposal ceremony (مجلس خواستگاری). Page: 32.2×20.4 cm, frame: 30.9×18.8 cm. The Persian numerals ۱۱ (11) are written in pencil in the upper left margin. This folio is associated with nos. 6, 4, 10, 2.

Or. 27.133 (2): 13: Tahmuras III. Page: 32.3×20.2 cm, frame: 32.3×18.8 cm.

Or. 27.133 (2): 14: A young couple being entertained by musicians and dancers. Page: 32.3×20.2 cm, frame: 30.8×18.8 cm. The Persian numeral ۴ (4) is written in pencil in the upper left margin.

Or. 27.133 (2): 15: Zahak V.[71] Page: 20.5×32.1 cm, frame: 30.9×18.8 cm (see no. 51).

Or. 27.133 (2): 16: Lovers enjoying a performance. Page: 32.1×20.5 cm, frame. 30.8×18.7 cm. The Persian numeral ۶ (6) is written in pencil in the upper left margin.

Or. 27.133 (2): 17: Faridun VI. Page: 32.3×20.4 cm, frame: 30.8×18.7 cm (see no. 54).

Or. 27.133 (2): 18: A young couple being entertained by musicians and dancers. Page: 32.3×20.5 cm, frame: 30.8×18.7 cm. The Persian numeral ۸ (8) is written in pencil in the upper left margin.

Or. 27.133 (2): 19: Jamshid IV. Page: 32.1×20 cm, frame: 30.8×18.8 cm.

Or. 27.133 (2): 20: The scene of a love affair. Page: 32.1×20 cm, frame: 30.9×18.8 cm. What appears to be the Persian numeral ۵ (5) is written in pencil in the upper left margin. This folio is associated with no. 24 and no. 38.

Or. 27.133 (2): 21: Ardashir I. Page: 32.8×20.4 cm, frame: 30.9×18.8 cm (see no. 42).

Or. 27.133 (2): 22: A baby's birth and celebration. Page: 32.8×20.4 cm, frame: 30.9×18.8 cm. The Persian numerals ۲۳ (23) are written in pencil in the upper left margin. This folio is associated with nos. 8, 36, 40.

Or. 27.133 (2): 23: Iraj, Sam and Tur, three sons of Faridun. Page: 32.2×20.5 cm, frame: 30.8×18.8 cm.

Or. 27.133 (2): 24: The discovery of the affair. Page: 32.2×20.5 cm, frame: 30.8×18.8 cm. The Persian numeral ٧ (7) is written in pencil in the upper left margin.

Or. 27.133 (2): 25: Humay VII, the daughter of Bahman. Page: 32.3×20.4 cm (see no. 56).

Or. 27.133 (2): 26: Food being prepared for a banquet. Page: 20.4×32.3 cm, frame: 18.8×30.9 cm. The Persian numerals ١٩ (19) are written in pencil in the upper left margin.

Or. 27.133 (2): 27: Kayumars. Paper: 20.5×32.1 cm, frame: 30.8×18.7 cm (see no. 63).

Or. 27.133 (2): 28: Kebab shop. Paper: 20.5×32.1 cm, frame: 30.8×18.7 cm. The Persian numeral ١ (1) is written in pencil in the upper left margin.

Or. 27.133 (2): 29: Bahman VI. Page: 20.4×32.8 cm, frame: 18.8×30.9 cm (see no. 50).

Or. 27.133 (2): 30: Public amusement. Page: 20.4×32.8 cm, frame: 30.9×18.8 cm. The number ١٧ (17) is written in pencil in the upper left margin.

Or. 27.133 (2): 31: Darab VIII. Page: 20.4×32.4 cm, frame: 18.8×31 cm (see no. 53).

Or. 27.133 (2): 32: Fire play to accompany the newlyweds to their home. Page: 32.4×20.4 cm, frame: 18.7×30.4 cm. The Persian numeral ٢ (2) is written in pencil in the upper left margin.

Or. 27.133 (2): 33: Siyamak. Page: 19.9×32.8 cm, frame: 18.8×30.9 cm (see no. 77).

Or. 27.133 (2): 34: Stealing the Mulla Nasruddin's donkey. Page: 19.9×32.3 cm, frame: 18.8×30.9 cm. The Persian numeral ٢ (2) is written in pencil in the upper left margin.

Or. 27.133 (2): 35: Shapur II. Page: 19.9×32.3 cm, frame: 18.8×32.6 cm (see no. 73).

Or. 27.133 (2): 36: Rite of circumcision and accompanying celebration. Page: 19.9×32.3 cm, frame: 18.8×32.6 cm. The Persian numerals ٢٤ (24) are written in pencil in the upper left margin. This folio is associated with nos. 8, 22, 40.

Or. 27.133 (2): 37: Manuchir VII. Paper 32.1×20.9 cm, frame: 30.8×18.7 cm (see no. 67).

Or. 27.133 (2): 38: A culprit with a string through his nose, led through the bazaar.[72] Paper: 32.1×20.9 cm, frame: 30.8×18.7 cm. The Persian numeral ٩ (9) is written in pencil in the upper left margin. The number 117 is written in Western numerals in the upper right margin.

Or. 27.133 (2): 39: Probably Hurmuz III. Paper: 32.3×26 cm, frame: 30.20×18.8/9 cm (see no. 59).

Or. 27.133 (2): 40: A scene of schoolboys. Paper: 32.3×26 cm, frame: 30.20×18.8/9 cm. The Persian numerals ٢٥ (25) are written in pencil in the upper left margin. The note "T9" is written in pencil in the lower margin. This folio is associated with nos. 8, 22, 36.

Or. 27.133 (2): 41: Dara IX. Paper: 32.3×20.5 cm, frame: 31×19 cm (see no. 52).

Or. 27.133 (2): 42: Ardashir I. Page: 20.1×16 cm. There are two Persian notes, one in ink and one in pencil, which say اردشیر (Ardashir) (see no. 21).

Or. 27.133 (2): 43: Ardashir X. Page: 20.2×16 cm. There are two Persian notes, one in ink and one in pencil, which say اردشیر (Ardashir).

Or. 27.133 (2): 44: Azarmidokht XXVII. Page: 20.4×16 cm. There are two Persian notes, one in ink and one in pencil, which say آذرمیدخت (Azarmidokht).

Or. 27.133 (2): 45: Bahram VI. Page: 20.1×16 cm. There are two Persian notes, one in ink and one in pencil, which say بهرام (Bahram).

Or. 27.133 (2): 46: Bahram XIV. Page: 20.1×16 cm. There are two Persian notes, one in ink and one in pencil, which say بهرام (Bahram).

Or. 27.133 (2): 47: Bahram XII. Page: 16.1×20.2 cm. There are two Persian notes, one in ink and one in pencil, which say بهرام (Bahram).

Or. 27.133 (2): 48: Bahram V. Page: 22×16 cm. There are two Persian notes, one in ink and one in pencil, which say بهرام (Bahram).

Or. 27.133 (2): 49: Bahram IV. Page: 20×16 cm. There are two Persian notes, one in ink and one in pencil, which say بهرام (Bahram).

Or. 27.133 (2): 50: Bahman VI. Page: 20.4×16 cm. There are two Persian notes, one in ink and one in pencil, which say بهمن (Bahman) (see no. 29).

Or. 27.133 (2): 51: Zahak V. Page: 20.3×16 cm. There are two Persian notes, one in ink and one in pencil, which say ضحاک مار بردوش (Zahak, the snake-shouldered) and ضحاک (Zahak).

Or. 27.133 (2): 52: Dara IX. Page: 20.3×16 cm. There are two Persian notes, one in ink and one in pencil, which say دارا (Dara).

Or. 27.133 (2): 53: Darab VIII. Page: 16×20.3 cm. There are two Persian notes, one in ink and one in pencil, which say داراب (Darab).

Or. 27.133 (2): 54: Faridun VI. Page: 20.2×16 cm. There are two Persian notes, one in ink and one in pencil, which say فریدون (Faridun).

Or. 27.133 (2): 55: Firuz XVII. Page: 16.1×20.2 cm. There are two Persian notes, one in ink and one in pencil, which say فیروز (Firuz).

Or. 27.133 (2): 56: Humay VII, the daughter of Bahman. Page: 20.1×16 cm. There are two Persian notes, one in ink and one in pencil, which say هما (Huma).

Or. 27.133 (2): 57: Hurmuz XXI. Page: 16×20.22 cm. There are two Persian notes, one in ink and one in pencil, which say هرمز (Hurmuz).

Or. 27.133 (2): 58: Hurmuz XVI. Page: 20.2×16.1 cm. There are two Persian notes, one in ink and one in pencil, which say هرمز (Hurmuz).

Or. 27.133 (2): 59: Hurmuz III. Page: 20.2×16.1 cm. There are two Persian notes, one in ink and one in pencil, which say هرمز (Hurmuz).

Or. 27.133 (2): 60: Hurmuz VIII. Page: 20.3×16.1 cm. There are two Persian notes, one in ink and one in pencil, which say هرمز (Hurmuz).

Or. 27.133 (2): 61: Hushang II. Page: 20.4×15.9 cm. There are two Persian notes, one in ink and one in pencil, which say هوشنگ (Hushang).

Or. 27.133 (2): 62: Alexander X. Page: 20.4×16. There are two Persian notes, one in ink and one in pencil, which say اسکندر (Iskandar).

Or. 27.133 (2): 63: Kayumars. Page: 20.4×16.1 cm. There are two Persian notes, one in ink and one in pencil, which say کیومرس (Kayumars).

Or. 27.133 (2): 64: Kay Kavus II. Page: 20.3×16 cm. There are two Persian notes, one in ink and one in pencil, which say کیکاوس (Kay Kavus).

Or. 27.133 (2): 65: Luhrasb IV. Page: 20.2×16 cm. There are two Persian notes, one in ink and one in pencil, which say لهراسب (Luhrasb).

Or. 27.133 (2): 66: Kay Gubad I. Page: 20.2×16.1 cm. There are two Persian notes, one in ink and one in pencil, which say کیقباد (Kay Gubad).

Or. 27.133 (2): 67: Manuchir VII. Page: 20×16. There are two Persian notes, one in ink and one in pencil, which say منوچهر (Manuchir).

Or. 27.133 (2): 68: Anushirvan (Nushirvan) XX. Page: 20.2×16.1 cm. There are two Persian notes, one in ink and one in pencil, which say نوشیروان (Nushirvan).

Or. 27.133 (2): 69: Shahrazad XXV. Page: 20.2×17/17.2 cm. There are two Persian notes, one in ink and one in pencil, which (mistakenly) say پلاش (Pelash).[73]

Or. 27.133 (2): 70: Purandukht XXVI. Page: 20.3×16.1 cm. There are two Persian notes, one in ink and one in pencil, which say پوراندخت (Purandukht).

Or. 27.133 (2): 71: Qubad XIX. Page: 20.2×18.8/9 cm. There are two Persian notes, one in ink and one in pencil, which say قباد and غباد (Qubad) (see no. 81r).

Or. 27.133 (2): 72: Shapur IX. Page: 20.2×16.1/2 cm. There are two Persian notes, one in ink and one in pencil, which say شاپور (Shapur).

Or. 27.133 (2): 73: Shapur II. Page: 20.22×16 cm. There are two Persian notes, one in ink and one in pencil, which say شاپور (Shapur).

Or. 27.133 (2): 74: Shapur XI. Page: 20.3×16/16.2 cm. There are two Persian notes, one in ink and one in pencil, which say شاپور (Shapur).

Or. 27.133 (2): 75: Shahrazad XXV. Page: 20.3×16.1 cm. It carries two notes that both say شهرآزاد (Shahrazad).

Or. 27.133 (2): 76: Shiruya XXIII. Page: 20.3×16 cm. There are two Persian notes, one in ink and one in pencil, which say شیرویه (Shiruya).

Or. 27.133 (2): 77: Siyamak. Page: 20.3×16 cm. There are two Persian notes, one in ink and one in pencil, which say سیامک (Siyamak).

Or. 27.133 (2): 78: Yazdgird XIII. Page: 20.3×16.1/2 cm. There are two Persian notes, one in ink and one in pencil, which say یزدگرد (Yazdgird).

Or. 27.133 (2): 79: Yazdgird XXIX. Page: 20.3×16 cm. There are two Persian notes, one in ink and one in pencil, which say یزدگرد (Yazdgird).

Or. 27.133 (2): 80: Zab and Garshasb. Page: 20.4×16. There are four Persian notes, in ink and in pencil, which say ذاب and ذابه (Zaba, Zab) and Garshasb (گرشاسب).

Or. 27.133 (2): 81r: Qubad XIX. Page: 20.1×14.9/15 cm.

Or. 27.133 (2): 81v: Yazdgird XV. Page: 20.1×14.9/15 cm. In the bottom right-hand corner, there is a note in Dutch in pencil that says "58 for 6" (*58 voor 6*).[74]

Or. 27.133 (2): 82: A man wearing a purple robe and holding a red ball in his hand. Page: 22.3×15.2/4 cm.

Or. 27.133 (2): 83: A man in purple attire. Page: 15.3×22.5 cm.

Or. 27.133 (2): 84: A man in a red robe with a long beard. Page: 17.4×11.3 cm.

Or. 27.133 (2): 85: A man in a red robe holding a red ball. Page: 22.3×15.2 cm.

Or. 27.133 (2): 86: A man in a red robe holding a red ball. Page: 22.4×15.4 cm.

Or. 27.133 (2): 87: A man in a red robe wearing a turban. Page: 22.3×15.1 cm.

Or. 27.133 (2): 88: A man in a red robe wearing a turban. Page: 22.4×15/15.1 cm.

Or. 27.133 (2): 89: A seated man in a red robe with a beard. Page: 22.4×15.1/14.9 cm.

Or. 27.133 (2): 90: A seated man in a red robe with a moustache. Page: 17.7×11.2 cm.

Or. 27.133 (2): 91: A seated man in a red robe with clasped hands. Page: 11.2×17.8 cm.

Or. 27.133 (2): 92: A seated serviceman. Page: 17.7×11.2 cm. The paper carries a Russian embossed stamp, on the left, below the figure.

Or. 27.133 (2): 93: A seated serviceman. Page: 17.8×11.2 cm.

Or. 27.133 (2): 94: A soldier with a spear in his hand. Page: 22.5×15 cm.

Or. 27.133 (2): 95: A standing man with a white turban. Page: 22.3×15.3 cm.

Or. 27.133 (2): 96: A standing man with a white turban. Page: 22.4×15.3 cm.

Or. 27.133 (2): 97: A young Qajar official in a chair. Page: c.19.2×11.2 cm.

Or. 27.133 (2): 98: A young Qajar official sits relaxed on the floor. Page: c.20.5×11.8 cm.

Or. 27.133 (2): 99: A young Qajar official sits relaxed on the floor. Page: 19.3×12.3 cm.

Or. 27.133 (2): 100: A moustachioed Qajar official in a chair. Page: 19.3×12.4 cm.

Or. 27.133 (2): 101: A young Qajar official holding a water pipe (*qalyan*). Page: 18.3/4×c.11.4 cm.

Or. 27.133 (2): 102: A young Qajar official holding a water pipe (*qalyan*). Page: 18.3×c.11.3 cm.

Or. 27.133 (2): 103: A young Qajar official holding a water pipe (*qalyan*). Page: 18.4×11.4 cm.

Or. 27.133 (2): 104: A Qajar official on horseback. Page: c.12×18.8 cm.

Or. 27.133 (2): 105: A Qajar official on horseback. Page: c.19×12.1 cm.

Or. 27.133 (2): 106: A Qajar man in Western attire on horseback. Page: c.19×12.1 cm.

Or. 27.133 (2): 107: A woman wearing a chador and orange pantaloons. Page: c.18×c.11.3 cm.

Or. 27.133 (2): 108: A woman wearing a chador and orange pantaloons. Page: 17.8×11.2 cm.

Or. 27.133 (2): 109: A woman wearing a chador and green pantaloons. Page: c.18.4×c.12.3 cm.

Or. 27.133 (2): 110: A woman seated with her legs crossed, holding a fan. Page: 17.9×11.1 cm.

Or. 27.133 (2): 111: A woman seated with her legs crossed, holding a fan. Page: 18×11.2 cm.

Or. 27.133 (2): 112: A woman seated with her legs crossed, holding a fan. Page: c.18×11.2 cm.

Or. 27.133 (2): 113: A woman seated with her legs crossed, holding a fan. Page: c.11.3×17.8 cm.

Or. 27.133 (2): 114: A woman seated with her legs crossed, holding a fan. Page: 17.8×c.11.2 cm.

Or. 27 133 (2): 115: A woman seated with her legs crossed, holding a fan. Page: c.17.9×c.11.1 cm.

Or. 27.133 (2): 116: A woman seated with her legs crossed, holding a fan. Page: c.17.7×c.11.1 cm.

Or. 27.133 (2): 117r: A woman seated with her legs crossed, holding a fan. Page: c.17.8×c.11 cm.

Or. 27.133 (2): 117v: Unfinished sketch of a horse. Page: c.17.8×c.11 cm.

Or. 27.133 (2): 118: A dancing girl plays the tambourine. Page: c.17.9×c.11.3 cm.

Or. 27.133 (2): 119: A dancing girl plays the tambourine. Page: c.18.4×11.5 cm.

Or. 27.133 (2): 120: A dancing girl plays the tambourine. Page: c.18.3×11.3 cm.

Or. 27.133 (2): 121: A dancing girl in a pink skirt plays the tambourine. Page: c.18.5×c.11.6 cm.

Or. 27.133 (2): 122: A dancing girl plays the tambourine. Page: 18.4×c.11.6 cm.

Or. 27.133 (2): 123: A dancing girl plays the goblet drum (*tombak*). Page: c.17.5×c.11.3 cm.

Or. 27.133 (2): 124: A young woman in a pink blouse dances. Page: 21.3×17.3 cm.

Or. 27.133 (2): 125: A young woman in a yellow blouse dances. Page: 21.3×17.2 cm.

Or. 27.133 (2): 126: A young woman in a pink blouse dances. Page: Page: 21.3×17.3 cm.

Or. 27.133 (2): 127: A woman in a yellow blouse poses holding a wine glass. Page: 21.4×17 cm.

Or. 27.133 (2): 128: A woman in an orange blouse poses holding a wine glass. Page: 21.1×17.2 cm.

Or. 27.133 (2): 129: A seated woman in a blue skirt poses holding a glass. Page: 21.3×17.3 cm.

Or. 27.133 (2): 130: A dancing girl plays the tambourine. Page: 21.5×17.2 cm.

Or. 27.133 (2): 131: A dancing girl plays the goblet drum (*tombak*). Page: 21.3×17.3 cm.

Or. 27.133 (2): 132: A dancing girl in a pink skirt plays the goblet drum (*tombak*). Page: 21.3×17.3 cm.

Or. 27.133 (2): 133: A dancing girl in a yellow blouse plays the tambourine. Page: 21.3×17.3 cm.

Or. 27.133 (2): 134: A seated girl plays the dulcimer (*santur*). Page: 21.4×17.3 cm.

Or. 27.133 (2): 135: A seated woman looks at herself in a mirror. Page: 21.4×17.3 cm.

Or. 27.133 (2): 136: A woman in a chador and red pantaloons. Page: 21.2×17.3 cm.

Or. 27.133 (2): 137: A woman in a chador and green pantaloons. Page: 21.4×17.4 cm.

Or. 27.133 (2): 138: A young woman in a yellow blouse. Page: 17.2×11.2 cm.

Or. 27.133 (2): 139: A young woman in a yellow blouse. Page: 17.8×11.3 cm.

Or. 27.133 (2): 140: A young woman in a yellow blouse. Page: 17.7×11.2 cm.

Or. 27.133 (2): 141: A young woman in a yellow blouse. Page: 17.8×11.2 cm.

Or. 27.133 (2): 142: A dancing girl plays the tambourine. Page: 16.8×10.4 cm.

Or. 27.133 (2): 143: A barber shop (*dalak*).[75] Page: 17.9×11.3 cm.

Or. 27.133 (2): 144: A farm worker. Page: 17.9×11.1 cm.

Or. 27.133 (2): 145: A working man. Page: 18×11.3 cm.

Or. 27.133 (2): 146: A vegetable vendor. Page: 17.8×11.2 cm.

Or. 27.133 (2): 147: A youth holding an *esfand* (Peganum harmala) incense burner.[76] Page: 18×11.3 cm.

Or. 27.133 (2): 148: A pigeon fancier.[77] Page: 18×11.4 cm.

Or. 27.133 (2): 149: A kitchen assistant. Page: 17.8×11.5 cm.

Or. 27.133 (2): 150: A farm worker. Page: 17.7×11 cm.

Or. 27.133 (2): 151: A goblet-drum (*tombak*) player. Page: 17.8×11.2 cm.

Or. 27.133 (2): 152: A young man plays the *naqqarah*. Page: 17.8×11.2 cm.

Or. 27.133 (2): 153: An entertainer with a sword. Page: 17.8×11.2 cm.

Or. 27.133 (2): 154: An ironer. Page: 17.9×11.1 cm (see no. 174).

Or. 27.133 (2): 155: A man exercises with *kabbada* at the *zurkhana*.[78] Page: 11.4×17.9 cm.

Or. 27.133 (2): 156: A man exercises with an Indian club (میل) at the *zurkhana*. Page: 11.4×17.9 cm.

Or. 27.133 (2): 157: Two buffoons. Page: 17.8×11.2 cm.

Or. 27.133 (2): 158: A yellow-capped jester. Page: 17.8×c.11.3 cm.

Or. 27.133 (2): 159: A snake charmer. Page: 17.9×11.3 cm.

Or. 27.133 (2): 160: An entertainer on a wild goat. Page: 17.7×c.11.2 cm.

Or. 27.133 (2): 161: An entertainer on a lion with a snake in his hands. Page: c.17.8×10.9 cm.

Or. 27.133 (2): 162: An entertainer on a donkey. Page: 17.7×11.1 cm.

Or. 27.133 (2): 163: An entertainer with a red cap and a dog. Page: 17.9×11.5 cm.

Or. 27.133 (2): 164: An entertainer rehearsing with a monkey (*luti antari*). Page: 17.8×11.1 cm.

Or. 27.133 (2): 165: An entertainer with a yellow cap rehearsing with a dog. Page: 17.9×c.11.1 cm.

Or. 27.133 (2): 166: An entertainer with two snakes sitting on a lion. Page: 21.3×c.17.2 cm.

Or. 27.133 (2): 167: A black entertainer holding a snake sitting on a lion. Page: c.17.3×21.4 cm.

Or. 27.133 (2): 168: A greengrocer's shop. Page: 18.5×16.1 cm, painting: 16.9×12.9 cm.

Or. 27.133 (2): 169: A leather-bucket maker. Page: 18.4×16.3, painting: 16×11.6 cm.

Or. 27.133 (2): 170: A seller of rice and soup. Page: 18.5×14.9, painting: 15.9×11.8 cm.

Or. 27.133 (2): 171: A butcher's shop. Page: c.18.5×16.1, painting: 16.1×11.5 cm.

Or. 27.133 (2): 172: A shop in the bazaar. There is a Persian inscription at the bottom, the middle of which is partially readable: '...shop' (... خانه).[79] Paper: 18.5×16.3 cm, painting: 15.8×11.8 cm.

Or. 27.133 (2): 173: A blacksmith's shop. Page: 19.3×16.1 cm, painting: 17.5×13.2 cm.

Or. 27.133 (2): 174: A pressing and ironing shop. Page: c.18.5×16.1 cm, painting: 16.3×c.11.2 cm.

Or. 27.133 (2): 175: A crystal (glassware) shop. There is a Persian note that reads 'crystal shop' (دکان بلور فروشی). Paper: 18.3×15.3 cm, painting: c.14.3×10 cm.

Or. 27.133 (2): 176: A barber performs bloodletting on a woman. Page: c.18.6×16.2 cm, painting: 15.3×11.4 cm.

Or. 27.133 (2): 177: A bakery. Page: 19.5×16.3 cm, painting: c.18×c.14.5 cm.

Or. 27.133 (2): 178: A brass shop (mortars, braziers, candlesticks). Page: 18×c.14.3 cm, painting: c.10.2×14.5 cm.

Or. 27.133 (2): 179: A woman at the comber's shop. There is a Persian note at the bottom, centre: 'a comber's shop' (دکان حلاجی). Page: c.16×12.5 cm, painting: 10.3×14.5 cm.

Or. 27.133 (2): 180: A retailer shop. Page: 18.4×16.3 cm, painting: 11.8×16 cm. The folio bears a Persian note, which is partially readable: 'the shop of ....' (دکان ... فروشی).[80]

Or. 27.133 (2): 181: Children standing in front of the marionette puppet shop (*khayma shab bazi*). Page: 16.3×18 cm, painting: 15.7×c.11.9 cm.

Or. 27.133 (2): 182: Builders. Page: 21.9×c.15 cm.

Or. 27.133 (2): 183: A man on camelback. Page: c.17×c.14.5 cm.

Or. 27.133 (2): 184: A yoghurt seller. Page: c.23.4×14.3 cm.

Or. 27.133 (2): 185: A dervish. Page: 19.3×16.1 cm.

Or. 27.133 (2): 186: A mulla. Page: 15.7×14.6 cm.

Or. 27.133 (2): 187: A secretary (*mirza*).[81] Page: c.16×14.2 cm.

Or. 27.133 (2): 188: A dervish smoking a *chibouk*. Page: 16.7×10.6 cm.

Or. 27.133 (2): 189: A man dozes off as a page fans him. Page: 18.3×12.7 cm.

Or. 27.133 (2): 190: A girl in a white blouse plays the tambourine. Page: 18.6×12.5 cm.

Or. 27.133 (2): 191: A young man hunts a wild boar. Page: 18.6×12.5 cm.

Or. 27.133 (2): 192: A man in a grey robe smoking a *chibouk*. Page: 17.9×12.8 cm.

Or. 27.133 (2): 193: A dervish smokes a water pipe, while a maid serves him food. Page: 18.3×13.1 cm.

Or. 27.133 (2): 194: A young man relaxes while looking at the scenery. Page: 17.4×10.3 cm.

Or. 27.133 (2): 195: Two seated dervishes. Page: 20.5×13.3 cm.

Or. 27.133 (2): 196: A young gentleman on horseback. Page: 18.5×13.2 cm.

Or. 27.133 (2): 197: Two gazelles. Page: 16.6×c.10.1 cm.

Or. 27.133 (2): 198: A young man hunts a gazelle. Page: 20.7×13.1 cm.

Or. 27.133 (2): 199: A hunter with a rifle. Page: 16.3×10.2 cm.

Or. 27.133 (2): 200: An elephant with a howdah. Page: 17.8×11.1 cm.

Or. 27.133 (2): 201: A woman on horseback looking at a panorama. Page: 18×12.7 cm.

Or. 27.133 (2): 202: A woman on horseback looking at a panorama. Page: 18.6×12.6 cm.

Or. 27.133 (2): 203: A woman on horseback. Page: 17.9×11.3 cm.

Or. 27.133 (2): 204: Two men conversing. Page: 16.2×10.2 cm.

Or. 27.133 (2): 205: A seated young dervish with a cup of wine. Page: 15.7×9.8 cm.

Or. 27.133 (2): 206: A gentleman. The note "T5" is written at the bottom right. Page: 17.1×10.5 cm.

Or. 27.133 (2): 207: A seated maid. Page: 17.1×c.10.6 cm.

Or. 27.133 (2): 208: Two ducks. Page: 20.3×13.3 cm.

Or. 27.133 (2): 209: A rooster. Page: 16.5×10.4 cm.

Or. 27.133 (2): 210: A rooster. Page: 18.2×c.12.4 cm.

Or. 27.133 (2): 211: A hawk sits with its wings outspread. Page: 9.6×13.1 cm.

Or. 27.133 (2): 212: An eagle hunts a mallard. Page: c. 20.2×c.13.2 cm.

Or. 27.133 (2): 213: A hawk on a perch. Page: 21.2×13.8 cm.

Or. 27.133 (2): 214: A grey saluki. Page: 31.6×c.10.1 cm.

Or. 27.133 (2): 215: A brown saluki. Page: 13.3×c.10.3 cm.

Or. 27.133 (2): 216: A saluki with a stick in its mouth. Page: 15×10.1 cm.

Or. 27.133 (2): 217: A saluki with a stick in its mouth. Page: 21.5×13.6 cm.

Or. 27.133 (2): 218: A lion biting into its prey's thigh. Page: c.21.4×13 cm.

Or. 27.133 (2): 219: A lion biting into its prey's thigh. Page: c.18.4×12.8 cm.

Or. 27.133 (2): 220: Camel fight. Page: 19.1×13.7 cm.

Or. 27.133 (2): 221: A camel with a blue saddle. Page: c.17.5×11 cm.

Or. 27.133 (2): 222: A goat. Page: 16.2×10.3 cm.

Or. 27.133 (2): 223: A cow. Page: c.17.8×11.3 cm.

Or. 27.133 (2): 224: A rose branch and butterfly. Page: 21.3×13.5 cm.

Or. 27.133 (2): 225: An iris. Page: 22.7×c.14.9 cm.

Or. 27.133 (2): 226: A bird perched on a rose branch. Page: c.21.1×17.2 cm.

Or. 27.133 (2): 227: A bird perched on a branch full of blossoms. Page: 21.2×17.1 cm.

Or. 27.133 (2): 228 r: A bird perched on a flower with a violet blossom. Page: 21.2×17 cm.

Or. 27.133 (2): 228 v: A bird perched on the branch of a cherry tree in bloom. Page: 21.2×17.2 cm.

Or. 27.133 (2): 229: Three birds perched on the branch of a tree. Page: 21.4×15.4 cm.

Or. 27.133 (2): 230: Pears on a tree. Page: 17.9×11.3 cm.

Or. 27.133 (2): 231: The Lion and the Sun (*Shir u Khurshid*), Page: 40.2×30 cm. There is a note in pencil at the bottom right that reads "T7".

Or. 27.133 (2): 232: A woman and a parrot. Page: 30×20.2 cm.

Or. 27.133 (2): 233. A girl in a purple dress holding a rose. Page: 20.5×c.30 cm.

Or. 27.133 (2): 234: A girl in a purple skirt holding flowers. Page: 15×10.2 cm.

Or. 27.133 (2): 235: A man in an Ottoman army uniform with a sword. Page: c.35×21 cm.

Or. 27.133 (2): 236: A girl and an Ottoman serviceman. Page: 30×20 cm.

Or. 27.133 (2): 237: A dervish with a beggar's bowl (*kashkul*), an axe (*tabarzin*), and a rose. Page: c.30×20.7 cm. There is a scratched-out note in pencil at the bottom right, which reads "T[...]".

Or. 27.133 (2): 238: A warrior on horseback with a spear. Page: 30.1×20.3 cm. There is a note in pencil at the bottom right that reads "T10".

Or. 27.133 (2): 239: Suhrab on horseback ready for battle. Page: 34.5×21.5 cm. There is a Persian note that reads سهراب (Suhrab).

Or. 27.133 (2): 240: A man on horseback hunting. Page: 32.5×22 cm.

Or. 27.133 (2): 241: Rostam and the White Div (Demon). Page: 33.5×c.22 cm. There is a Persian note that reads رستم و دیو سفید (Rostam and the White Div).

Or. 27.133 (2): 242: The crew of an Ottoman ship. Page: 32.5×21.5 cm.

Or. 27.133 (2): 243: Two men in a carriage. Page: 33×21 cm.

Or. 27.133 (2): 244: A man in a carriage wearing a crown and holding a rose. Page: 33.5×21.5 cm.

Or. 27.133 (2): 245: An entertainer with an animal. Page: 15.2×10 cm.

Or. 27.133 (2): 246: A local animal.[82] Page: c.14.6×10 cm.

Or. 27.133 (2): 247: A calligraphy of the Qur'anic maxim, نصرمن الله و فتح قریب (Support from Allah, and imminent victory).[83] Page: 32.5×20.5 cm.

Appendix: Watermarks from the Hotz painting collection

The photographs were taken by the author in January 2025.

Several watermarks show up throughout the collection. Examples, from left to right: top: nos. 62, 208; bottom: nos. 191, 217.

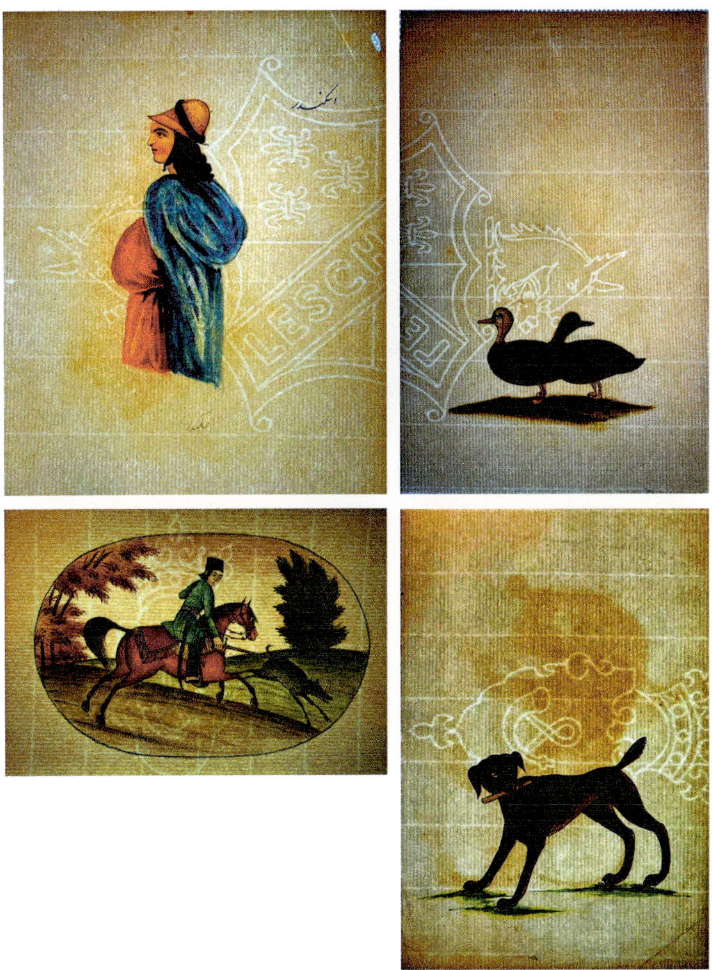

In Set I, all the folios carry the full watermark. In this set, with the exception of the bi-folio nos. 35-36, the historical protagonist is depicted on the sheet with the watermark of a bust of a donkey, with the date of 1875 below the figure. The joined folio bears the watermark of a countermark with a circle bearing an inscription, surmounted by an imperial crown (see chapter 4, page 1). Example, bi-folio nos. 39-40.

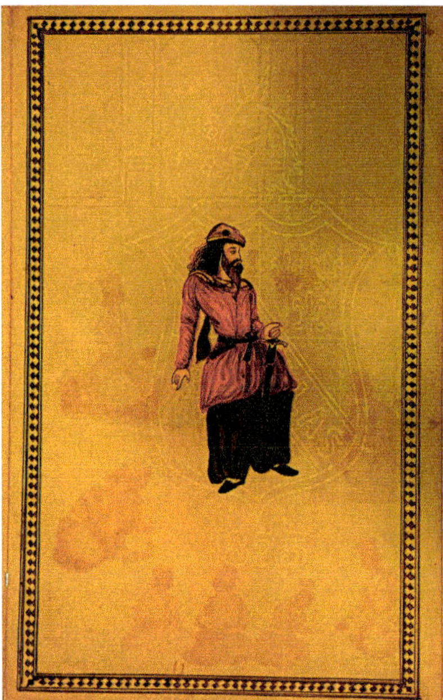
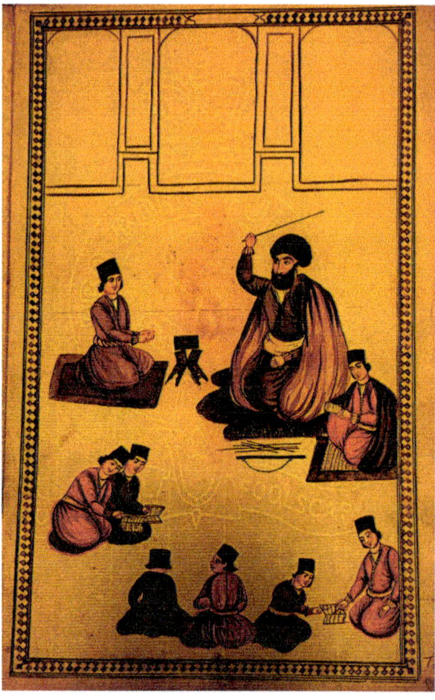

In some instances, the full watermark can be seen by joining together two paintings. Examples, from left to right: top: no. 228 (r), (v); bottom: nos. 130, 127.

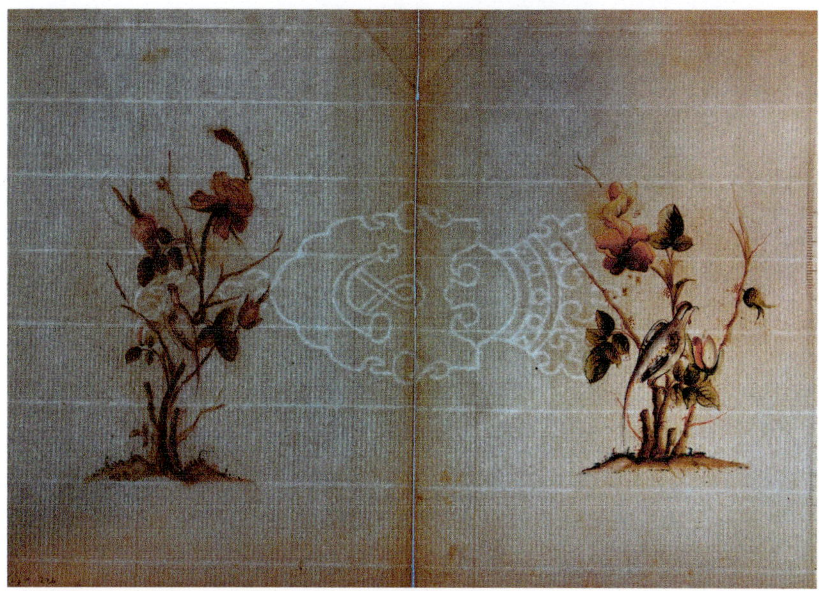

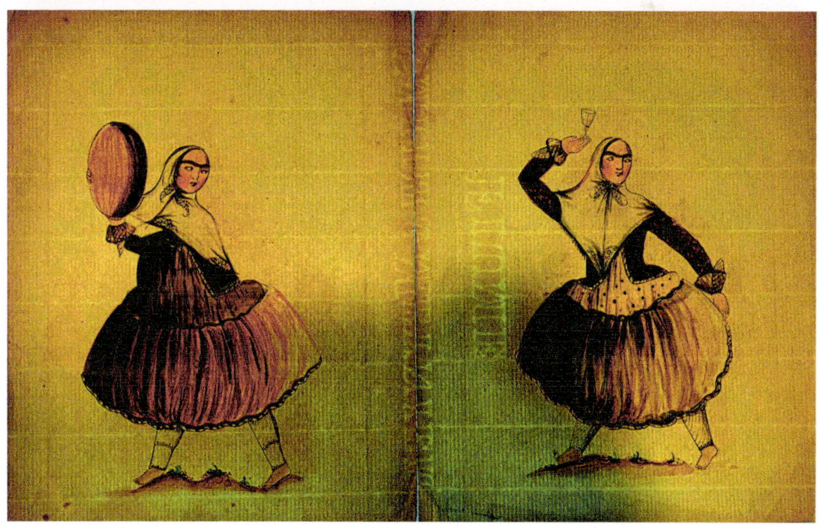

Selection of other watermarks. Examples, from left to right: nos. 206, 224.

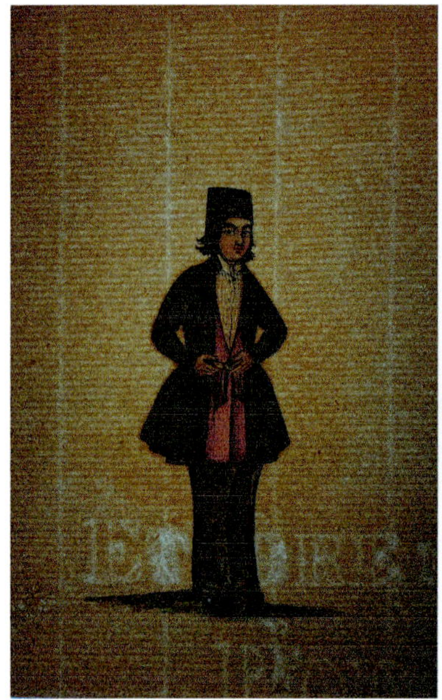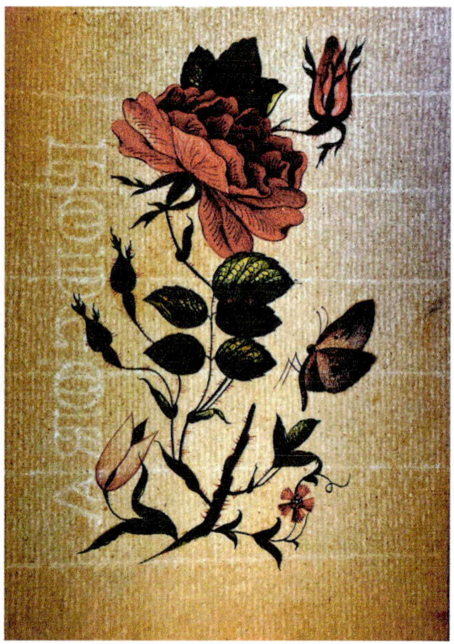

Notes

1   On the biography of Hotz and his career in Persia, see Floor, W. & Sajadi, F., "Albert Hotz: Irandust, mover & shaker", in *The Dutch in Persia and The Persians among the Dutch (1789-1925)* (forthcoming). Engelberts, Th.H.E., *A Persian from a Distant Land* (The Hague: 2000). Floor, W., "Hotz versus Muḥammad Shafī: A Case Study in Commercial Litigation in Qājār Iran, 1888-1894", *International Journal of Middle East Studies* 15.2 (1983), 185-209, Floor, W. & Abu Turabiyan, B., "Bungah-daran va Maghazi-daran-i Hollandi dar Iran-i Qajar", *Pajuhish-hayi Ulum Tarikhi* 7.1 (1394/2015), 79-131. Also, his career is mentioned in several publications related to his photograph collection; see notes 4, 5.

2   "Hotz & Co.", *Nieuwe Amsterdamsche Courant, Algemeen Handelsblad*, 02-09-1875, no. 13904, Supplement: Advertising, no. 31159.

3   "From Today's Javanese Newspaper", *Java-bode: nieuws, handels- en advertentieblad voor Nederlandsch-Indie*, 10-09-1875, no. 213, 25th year.

4   The Hotz Collection comprises approximately 5,000 printed books, along with 23 albums and portfolios containing around 1,300 photographs. Vuurman, C., *Nineteenth-Century Persia in the Photographs of Albert Hotz: Images from the Hotz photograph collection of Leiden University Library, the Netherlands* (Rotterdam: 2011). Witkam, J.J., "Albert Hotz and his photographs of Iran: An introduction to the Leiden Collection", in Islami, K. (ed.), *Iran and Iranian Studies. Essays in Honor of Iraj Afshar* (Princeton: 1998), 276-287. Vuurman, C. & Martens, Th., *Perzië en Hotz: beelden uit de fotocollectie-Hotz in de Leidse Universiteitsbibliotheek: catalogus bij een tentoonstelling in de Leidse Universiteitsbibliotheek van 30 januari tot 4 maart 1995 (Ramadan tentoonstelling 1415)* (Leiden: 1995). Also, see Leiden University Libraries Collection Guides, *Albertus Paulus Hermanus Hotz archive and collection*: https://collectionguides.universiteitleiden.nl/resources/ubl063.

5   Vuurman, C., "'Greetings from Shiraz, the city of the purest air and clearest sky in the world': Ordinary Pictorial Delights from the Collections of Leiden University Library", *History of Photography: The First Hundred Years of Iranian Photography* 37.1 (2013), 32-47. Vuurman, C. & Barjesteh van Waalwijk van Doorn, F., "Vividly Painted Watercolours: Artistic Purchases from Persian Bazaars", *Qajar Studies: Journal of the International Qajar Studies Association* 12/13 (2013), 53-141.

6   This small group of Chinese paintings is not included in the present catalogue. It is noteworthy that Chinese pith paintings often depict subject matters similar to those found in Hotz's Qajar paintings; everyday life, ceremonies, entertainment, professions, flora, and fauna. Between the 1820s and 1860s, the market for these paintings flourished, largely due to growing interest and demand from Western collectors.

7   Qajar art—particularly its painting tradition—has been the subject of a rich body of scholarship, authored by numerous distinguished researchers. See Gwenaëlle, F. & Guillaume, C. (eds.), *Revealing the Unseen: New perspectives on Qajar art* (London & Paris: 2021), Diba, L. & Ekhtiar, M. (eds.), *Royal Persian Paintings: The Qajar Epoch 1785-1925* (London & New York: 1972). On lithography in the Qajar period, see Marzolph, U. & Zenhari, R., *Mirzā 'Ali-Qoli Kho'i: The Master Illustrator of Persian Lithographed Books in the Qajar Period*, 2 vols. (Leiden & Boston: 2022).

8   Exposition internationale, *Catalogue officiel de l'exposition internationale, coloniale et d'exportation générale d'Amsterdam, 1883* (Brussels: 1883), 264. See Persian sections: 307-310. To read about this exhibition, see Floor & Sajadi, "Albert Hotz".

9   Polak, J.E., *Description des articles exposés à l'Exposition internationale, coloniale et d'exportation générale d'Amsterdam 1883 par Perzische Handels-Vereeniging J.C.P. Hotz en Zoon, Rotterdam* (s.l.: 1883), 51.

10   "Perzië op de Tentoonstelling", *Nieuwe Amsterdamsche Courant, Algemeen Handelsblad*, 01-08-1883, no. 16738.

11   "Perzië", *Utrechtsch provinciaal en stedelijk dagblad*, 19-10-1883, no. 288.

12   The book was edited by Charles James Wills (died 1912), a British physician who served in Persia from 1866 to 1881. This book originally was published by James Justinian Morier (1782-1849) in 1824 in London. In 1897, Wills published his own edition of Morier's book. Wills embellished his version with several illustrations including some pieces of the collection of "his friend A. P. Hotz". The illustrations of this book will be discussed later on. Morier, J., *The adventures of Hajji Baba of Ispahan*, ed. Ch.J. Wills (London: 1897).

13   Dzucova, I.P., *Акоп Овнатанян: портреты – воспоминания о художнике, Akop Ovnatanjan: portrety – vospominanija o chudožnike* (Tbilisi: 2022), 413.

14   One of the few sources is the research of Karimzada Tabrizi, which I found imprecise: Karimzada Tabrizi, M.A., *Ahwal wa Asar-i Naqqashan-i Qadim-i Iran wa Barkhi az Mashahir-i Nigargar-i Hind wa Osmani*, vol. 1 (London: 1363/1985), 344-45.

15   Mumtahin al-Dawla, whose full name was Mirza Mahdi Khan Shaqaqi, studied architecture in France and is regarded as Persia's first modern architect.

16   Mumtahin al-Dawla, *Khatirat-i Mumtahin al-Dawla: Zindigi nama Mirza Mahdi Khan Mumtahin al-Dawla Shaqaqi*, H., Khanshqaqi (ed.) (Tehran: 1362/1983), 220. This book mentions that Mirza Muttalib owned some attic storage places (*balakhana*) in the bazaar of Tehran, located in Karwan Sarai of Haji Hassan Kulahduz; Ibid.

17   Ibid., 264 and 267.

18   Jalal al-Din Mirza Qajar, *Nama-i Khusrawan: Dastan-i Padishahan-i Pars bi Zaban-i Parsi ki Sudmand Marduman bivij-i Kudakan Ast: Nakhustin Nama, az Aghaz-i Abadiyan ta Anjam-i Sasanian* (Tehran: 1285/1868). *Nama-i Khusrawan* was supposed to be comprised of four volumes. The first volume, completed in 1868, covers the ancient history of Iran up to the end of the Sasanian dynasty (224 CE–650 CE). Amanat, A. &, Vejdani, F., "JALĀL-AL-DIN MIRZĀ", in *Encyclopædia Iranica*, vol. XIV. Fasc. 4 (1987), 405-410, available online: https://www.iranicaonline.org/articles/jalal-al-din-mirza.

19   By way of example, see the tile decorations of Gulistan Palace in Tehran, Tekiye Moaven al-molk in Kermanshah, the Kunstmuseum Den Haag (1053561, 1053563, and 1053565), Louvre Museum (MAO 682).

20   Exposition internationale, *Catalogue officiel*, 308. Mumtahin al-Dawla, *Khatirat-i*, 264 and 267. See note 21.

21   Muhammad Hassan Sani' al-Dawla I'timad al-Saltana, *Tarikh-i Muntazim-i Nasiri*, I. Rizvani (ed.), 3 vols. (Tehran: 1363/1984), 541, 1271, 2120.

22   Mu'ayyir al-Mamalik, D., "Rijal-i 'Asr-i Nasiri", *Yaghma* 108:4 (1957/1336), 170-71. While researching the Qajar sources on this painter, I came across another artist with a similar name, originally from Kashan. I have not been able to establish the authenticity of this source, nor the relationship between our painter and the Kashani. However, it may be useful for further study in the future. The source indicates that 'Abd al-Muttalib Kashani is a member of the famous Ghaffari family of artists, and that he is the nephew (sister's son) of Mirza Abu'l Hasan Khan Naqqash Bashi (1814-1866). 'Abd al-Muttalib travelled to Europe to study painting and returned from Italy in 1855/56, seven years later. See Mirza Tahir Munshi Isfahani, *Tazkira Ganj-i Shaygan* (Tehran: 1272/1855), 346-45.

23   I am grateful to Kianoosh Motaghedi for bringing this painting to my attention.

[24] Baines, J., "Watercolors Treatment on the Hotz's painting collection", unpublished report, available in archives of the Special Collections, Leiden University (Leiden: 2016-2017). See some information in Floor, W. & Couvrat-Desvergnes, A., *History of Paper in Iran, 1501-1925* (Washington, D.C.: 2022). Meanwhile, my study of this collection has yielded new insights, which I have incorporated into this text.

[25] Baines, "Watercolors Treatment", 39-40.

[26] See the paintings on a lavish mirror case dated to the second half of the nineteenth century, in the Khalili Collections (LAQ104). Likewise, "A pair of fine Qajar lacquer book covers depicting a wedding of Nasir al-Din Shah", d. 1846-1847, in Christie's auction, 21 April 2016, lot 137. "Six Qajar paintings", from the second half of the nineteenth century, in Bonhams auction, lot 88, 23 October 2018. Single artworks of note are fol. 28 and fol. 31 in the sketched folios of an album d. nineteenth century at the Harvard Art Museums (1960.161), and a painting of "A Persian Wedding", d. second half of the nineteenth century, in the National Museum of World Culture in Gothenburg (0000.00.0335), and "Wedding Procession", d. second half of the nineteenth century in the Museum of Islamic Art, Doha (MS. 772.2011.19). See the artworks in Khalili, N. D. & Robinson, B.W. & Stanley, T. & Bayani, M., *Lacquer of the Islamic Lands Pt. 2* (London: 1997), 44-45. To read about marriage customs in the Qajar period, see D'Allemagne, H.R., *Du Khorassan au pays des Backhtiaris, trois mois de voyage en Perse* (Paris: 1911), vol. 1, 200-209.

[27] See this particular scene executed on a mirror case, c. 1830-1850, in the Harvard Art Museums (2014.383).

[28] The adulterous love affair had been popular subject matter since the seventeenth century, and was usually depicted on a single page. In Qajar art, the scene of the affair or its aftermath was a favourite episode. In particular, it shows up in various illustrated/lithographed literary books such as *Anwar-i Suhayli* by Husayn Wa'iz Kashifi (1436-1504), *Tutinama* by Ziya' al-Din Nakhshabi (died 1350), and *Nan wa Halwa* by Sheikh Baha'i (1547-1621). See also Schwerda, M. X, "Amorous Couples: Depictions of Permitted and Prohibited Love", in Roxburgh, D. (eds.), *An Album of Artists' Drawings from Qajar Iran* (Cambridge, MA: 2017), 78-83.

[29] On street performance in the Qajar era, see Beyzai, B., *Namayish dar Iran (A Study on Iranian Theatre)* (Tehran: 1344/1965), 172-83; also see the relevant glossary, ibid., 226-42.

[30] "An unusual group of 38 album pages", d. late eighteenth/nineteenth century, in Bonhams auction, 29 March 2022, lot 130. This folio is in an album with other folios which have unrelated subject matters. The annotation is "Majlis-i Mulla Nasir al-Din" (the account of Mulla Nasir al-Din). To read about Mulla Nasruddin, see Javadi, H., "MOLLA NASREDDIN i. THE PERSON", in *Encyclopædia Iranica*, 15 July 2009, available online: https://www.iranicaonline.org/articles/molla-nasreddin-i-the-person; Marzolph, U., "Molla Nasr al-Din in Persia", *Iranian Studies* 28.3/4 (1995), 157-74.

[31] The story goes as follows: Once upon a time, Mulla and his monkey were passing through a desert. Two thieves came across him and plotted to steal his donkey. One of the thieves opened the bridle of the donkey and put it around his neck, and the second thief swiftly walked off with the donkey. Mulla continued on his way, unaware that a thief was walking beside him. After some time, he was startled to notice the man and asked, 'Who are you?'. The thief said 'Once I made a mistake, and God punished me by turning me into a donkey. Now please release me for the sake of my family'. Mulla sympathized with him and set him free. Days later, in the bazaar, Mulla came upon his donkey. Mulla approached him and said: 'One day you're a man, and the next day you're a donkey! What have you done wrong again?'. See the story and the cartoons in Tawfiq Kitabkhana (ed.), *Tawfiq Book: Mulla Nasruddin: the first illustrated collection of the famous jokes of 'Mulla' as the cartoon strip* (Negin: 1348/1969), n.p. This story can also be found in the *One Thousand and One Nights*; see Dawood, N.J. (trans.), *Tales from the Thousand and One Nights* (London & New York: 1973), 77-78.

32   Baines, "Watercolors Treatment", 43-44.

33   "Two standing portraits of Qajar Courtly Figures", c. 1880-1920, in Chiswick auctions, Islamic Art – Property of a European Collector Part VI, lot 29, 31 October 2023.

34   Baines, "Watercolors Treatment", 41.

35   There are a few other folios depicting women: nos. 190, 201, 202, 203, 207, 232, 233, 234.

36   "Two standing portraits of Qajar Courtly Figures", d. c. 1880-1920, in Chiswick auctions, Islamic Art – Property of a European Collector Part VI, lot 29, 31 October 2023.

37   For instance, see D'Allemagne, *Du Khorassan au pays des Backhtiaris*, vol. 2, 1-36. Wills, Ch.J., *In the land of the lion and sun; or Modern Persia. Being experiences of life in Persia from 1866 to 1881* (London: 1842), 40-41, 322-27.

38   1971-0107-0518 till 21, 1971-0107-0524, 1971-0107-0526, 1971-0107-0399. Jean Pozzi was the French plenipotentiary minister in Persia during 1935-1936. Habibi, N., "A Diplomat Collector: Jean Pozzi and His Persian Art Collection", in *Re-Orientations. Europe and Islamic art, from 1851 to today* (Zurich: 2013), 194-299.

39   Inventory numbers: 2006,0314,0.19 till 23. Of other samples, see Chekhab-Abudaya, M. & Sobers-Khan, N., *Qajar Women: Images of Women in 19th century Iran* (Exhibition Catalogue) (Doha: 2017).

40   The watermark is partly readable as "C R ...NTREM...". Baines, "Watercolors Treatment", 41.

41   The stamp is "ФАБРИКИ (factory in Russian) and three crescents. There are two words underneath which can be read as ПРОИЗВО АС (production as) МАРШЕВА, МАРШВВА or МАРШЗВА." Baines, "Watercolors Treatment", 44.

42   Idem, 42. Floor & Couvrat-Desvergnes, *History of paper in Iran*, 139.

43   Read the stamp of no. 144 in idem, 139.

44   See Massoudi, Sh., ""Kheimeh Shab Bazi": Iranian Traditional Marionette Theatre", *Asian Theatre Journal* 26.2 (2009), 260-80.

45   Starting in the sixteenth century, various bazaar scenes were conventionally depicted in the illuminated manuscripts of *Majalis al-'ushshaq*; from among the numerous examples, see a copy of this manuscript, d. 1552, in the Bodleian Library, MS. Ouseley Add. 24, ff. 44b, 46a, 78b, 120b. There is another copy of this manuscript in the National Library of France, Paris (Supplément Persan 1559), d. c. 1575, fols. 67v, 99r.

46   Read more about the bazaar in Wills, *In the Land of the Lion and Sun*, 188-94, and Tahwildar, Mirza Husayn Khan, *Jughrafiya-yi Isfahan*, M., Sotoudeh (ed.) (Tehran: 1342/1963), 92-127. See the English translation of the latter in Floor, W., *Guilds, Merchants, and Ulama in Nineteenth-century Iran* (Washington, D.C.: 2009), 159-212.

47   Morier, *The Adventures of Hajji Baba of Ispahan*. This book was originally published by James Justinian Morier (1782-1849) in 1824, and Wills published his own version in 1897. Wills's book is decorated with several illustrations from his collection, as well as some pieces from Hotz's collection.

48   To read about the contact between Hotz and Wills, see note 12. Also, see Engelberts, *A Persian from a Distant Land*, 39-41.

49   This album was previously at Sotheby's in London on 06.10.2010, lot 97. See Chekhab-Abudaya & Sobers-Khan, *Qajar Women: Images of Women*, 52-81.

50   Some of them have an inventory number (I B 9383, I B 9394, I B 9396, I B 9376, I B 9398, I B 9386).

51   For other artworks, see the album in the Professions Scrapbook, d. c. 1880, Gulistan Palace Library (1652), and also various folios in an album, d. c. 1850, at the British Museum (P&D 2001,0728.60).

52   The inscription on the stamp states: 'ТАТРОВСКОИ ПРОТАСЕЕВА ФАБРИКИ', Floor & Couvrat-Desvergnes, *History of paper in Iran*, 139.

53   Rochard, Ph. *The Zurkhāneh and Its Milieu: A Study of Traditional Athletics in Iran* (Boston, MA: 2025).

54   Wills, *In the Land of the Lion and Sun*, 306-309. D'Allemagne, *Du Khorassan au pays des Backhtiaris*, vol. 1, 160-73. Also, see Barjesteh van Waalwijk van Doorn, F., "Introduction to Entertainment in Qajar Persia", *Iranian Studies* 40.4 (2007), 447-54.

55   This artwork is a long painting, 352 cm in length, depicting various scenes. It belonged to Bertrand Hybennet (1846-1931), a Swedish dentist who served in the Qajar court from 1873 to 1907. His splendid collection has never been thoroughly studied. Suhrabi, B., "Early Swedish Travelers to Persia", *Iranian Studies* 38.4 (2005), 650-51. Among other examples, it is worth mentioning a fairly large nineteenth-century intestine decorated with entertaining scenes of animal and human acrobats, as well as dancers, preserved at the National Museum of Iran (8352). Also, see two folios in an album at the Museum of Islamic Art, Doha: Pahlivani Competition or Training (MS.722.2011.9) and Luti Antari (MS.722.2011.20), described in Chekhab-Abudaya & Sobers-Khan, *Qajar Women: Images of Women*, 55, 57.

56   Irina Dzucova has conducted an elaborate study on the biography and art of Akop Ovnatanjan; see Dzucova, *Акоп Овнатанян*, 303, 413.

57   Idem, 340.

58   Dzucova suggests that this occurred in 1861. In my opinion, this date is arguable. Idem, 304.

59   Floor, W. & Sajadi, F., *Khorshid Khanom: A Study in the Origin and Development of the Shir-o Khorshid Motif* (Washington, D.C.: 2024), 67-133.

60   Of the copious examples from the Qajar period, five folios from an album in the British Museum (1983,0315,0.1; fol. 21, 22, 24, 25, 26) are worthy of note.

61   A metal basin, made in 1285 in Cairo, Louvre Museum (OA 6316) or a fritware dish made in Syria, d. 1100s, preserved in the Cleveland Museum of Art (1938.7). This motif can also be found in Iran, for example on a terracotta tablet dated c. 1037-1194, found at Shadyakh (Nishapur) in Iran. Sheikhi, A. & Ghafarpoor, L., "Ramz-Gushai luh-i Sufali-yi Kashf Shudi az Muhavat-yi Islami-yi Shadiyakh-i Nishapur" (Decoding the Terracotta Tablet Found in the Shadyakh Islamic Site of Neishabour), *Fasl-nama Negareh* 33 (1393/2015) 32. Also, see Porter, V., & Rosser-Owen, M. (ed.), *Metalwork and Material Culture in the Islamic World: Art, Craft and Text. Essays presented to James W. Allan* (London & New York: 2012), 41-42.

62   Also, see this motif in a pen box decoration, d. c. 1830, in the Khalili Collections (LAQ163). Khalili, N.D. & Robinson, B.W. & Stanley, T., *Lacquer of the Islamic Lands Pt. 1* (London: 1993), 197.

63   Adamova, A., "The Iconography of a Camel Fight", *Muqarnas* 21.1 (1997), 1-14.

64   Masaharu Yoshida, *Safar-nama-yi Yusida Masaharu: naḵostin ferestada-yi Japon ba Iran dar dawra-yi Qajar, 1297-98 h.q.*, trans. H. Rajabzadeh (Tehran: 1994), 49.

65   Jentink, F.A., *Verslag omtrent het Rijks-Museum van Natuurlijke Historie te Leiden, Loopende Over het Tijdvak van 10 September 1891 tot 10 September 1982* (Leiden: 1892), 10.

66   I would cautiously read it as 'PODCORA'.

67   Floor & Sajadi, *Khorshid Khanom*, 67-133.

68   This term is found in al-Saff, the 61st Sura of the Qur'an, verse 13.

69   The names of people are taken from the book *Nama-i Khusrawan.*

70   I assume that this scene is part of a marriage genre series, and the ladies are handing out sweets in honour of the marriage proposal being accepted (بذل شیرینی مجلس).

71   In the corresponding lithograph in *Nama-i Khusrawan*, he does not have a snake on his shoulder. However, in this painting, Zahak has a rudimentary sketch of snakes on his shoulders, which the painter took from the folk and literary sources (including the text of *Nama-i Khusrawan*), where he is known as the snake-shouldered king. Jalal al-Din Mirza Qajar, *Nama-i Khusrawan*, 81-88.

72   I have borrowed the caption from Wills; see Morier, *The adventures of Hajji Baba of Ispahan*, 477.

73   See Jalal al-Din Mirza Qajar, *Nama-i Khusrawan*, 416.

74 I conjecture that this note was made by Hotz and refers to his deal for the number of artworks and their price. No currency is mentioned.

75 The *dalak*'s job included shampooing, shaving, and massaging, as well as bloodletting.

76 The practice of burning *esfand* seeds to ward off the evil eye is widely documented in early classical Persian literature. See Omidsalar, M., "ESFAND", in *Encyclopædia Iranica*, vol. VIII, Fasc. 6, 583-84, available online: https://iranicaonline.org/articles/esfand.

77 Wills, *In the Land of the Lion and Sun*, 94-95.

78 Idem, 98-99.

79 I cautiously conjecture that the full note reads *assarkhana* (اسارخانه), which is misspelled (عصار خانه). *Assarkhana* means the oil-miller workshop. I assume that this shop sells oils, such as grain, fruit, and vegetable oils.

80 I cautiously read it as 'a retailer' (دکان سقط فروشی).

81 Wills translates *mirza* as: "One who can write, a clerk, a secretary, a gentleman". Wills, *In the Land of the Lion and Sun*, 425.

82 I suspect that it is an Indian mongoose. For example, Wills wrote about a mongoose that lived in the Persian Gulf. He purchased one in Shiraz and kept it as a pet. Wills, *In the Land of the Lion and Sun*, 303.

83 This maxim is in al-Saff, the 61st sura of the Qur'an, verse 13.

Bibliography

Adamova, A., "The Iconography of A Camel Fight", *Muqarnas* 21.1 (1997), 1-14.

Amanat, A. &, Vejdani, F., "JALĀL-AL-DIN MIRZĀ", in *Encyclopædia Iranica*, vol XIV. Fasc. 4 (1987), 405-410, available online: https://www.iranicaonline.org/articles/jalal-al-din-mirza.

Baines, J., "Watercolors Treatment on the Hotz's painting collection", unpublished report in archive of the Special Collections, Leiden University (Leiden: 2016-2017).

Barjesteh van Waalwijk van Doorn, F., "Introduction to Entertainment in Qajar Persia, Iranian Studies", *Iranian Studies* 40.4 (2007), 447-54.

Beyzai, B., *Namayish dar Iran (A Study on Iranian Theatre)* (Tehran: 1344/1965).

Bonhams auction, "Six Qajar paintings", 23 October 2018, lot 88, https://www.bonhams.com/auction/24624/lot/88/six-qajar-paintings-depicting-preparations-before-a-wedding-the-ceremony-and-its-aftermath-persia-second-half-of-the-19th-century6/.

Bonhams auction, "An unusual group of 38 album pages", 29 March 2022, lot 130, https://www.bonhams.com/auction/27406/lot/130/an-unusual-group-of-38-album-pages-illustrating-scenes-from-firdausis-shahnama-nizamis-khamsa-jamis-haft-awrang-and-other-texts-persia-late-18th19th-century38/.

Chekhab-Abudaya, M. & Sobers-Khan, N., *Qajar Women: Images of Women in 19th century Iran* (Exhibition Catalogue) (Doha: 2017).

Chiswick auctions, "Two Standing Portraits of Qajar Courtly Figures", 31 October 2023, lot 29, https://www.chiswickauctions.co.uk/auction/lot/lot-29---two-standing-portraits-of-qajar-courtly-figures/?lot=232325&so=0&st=&sto=0&au=1047&ef=&et=&ic=False&sd=1&pp=96&pn=1&g=1.

Christie's auction, "A pair of fine Qajar lacquer book covers depicting a wedding of Nasir al-Din Shah", 21 April 2016, lot 137, https://www.christies.com/en/lot/lot-5985300.

D'Allemagne, H.R., *Du Khorassan au pays des Backhtiaris, trois mois de voyage en Perse*, 2 vols. (Paris: 1911).

Dawood, N.J. (trans.), *Tales from the Thousand and One Nights* (London & New York: 1973).

Diba, L. & Ekhtiar, M., (eds.), *Royal Persian Paintings: The Qajar Epoch 1785-1925* (London & New York: 1972).

Dzucova, I.P., *Акоп Овнатанян: портреты – воспоминания о художнике, Akop Ovnatanjan: portrety – vospominanija o chudožnike* (Tbilisi: 2022).

Engelberts, Th.H.E., *A Persian from a distant land* (The Hague: 2000).

Exposition internationale, *Catalogue officiel de l'exposition internationale, coloniale et d'exportation générale d'Amsterdam, 1883* (Bruxelles: 1883).

Feuvrier, J.B., *Trois ans à la cour de Perse* (Paris: 1900).

Floor, W., "Hotz versus Muḥammad Shafī: A Case Study in Commercial Litigation in Qājār Iran, 1888-1894", *International Journal of Middle East Studies* 15.2 (1983), 185-209.

Floor, W., "BLOODLETTING", in *Encyclopædia Iranica*, vol IV, Fasc. 3 (1989), 315-16, available online: https://www.iranicaonline.org/articles/bloodletting-ar.

Floor, W., *Guilds, Merchants, and Ulama in Nineteenth-century Iran* (Washington, D.C: 2009).

Floor, W. & Abu Turabiyan, B., "Bungah-daran va Maghazi-daran-i Hollandi dar Iran-i Qajar", *Pajuhish-hayi Ulum Tarikhi* 7.1 (1394/2015), 79-131.

Floor, W. & Couvrat-Desvergnes, A., *History of paper in Iran, 1501-1925* (Washington, D.C: 2022).

Floor, W. & Sajadi, F., *Khorshid Khanom: A Study in the Origin and Development of the Shir-o Khorshid Motif* (Washington, D.C: 2024).

Floor, W. & Sajadi, F., "Albert Hotz: Irandust, mover & shaker", in *The Dutch in Persia and The Persians among the Dutch (1789-1925)* (forthcoming).

"From Today's Javanese Newspaper", Java-bode: nieuws, handels- en advertentieblad voor Neder-landsch-Indie, 10-09-1875, no. 213, 25th year.

Gwenaëlle, F. & Guillaume, C. (eds.), *Revealing the unseen: new perspectives on Qajar art* (London & Paris: 2021).

Habibi, N., "A Diplomat Collector: Jean Pozzi and His Persian Art Collection", in *Re-Orientations. Europe and Islamic art, from 1851 to today* (Zurich: 2013), 194-299.

"Hotz & Co.", *Nieuwe Amsterdamsche Courant, Algemeen Handelsblad*, 02-09-1875, no. 13904, Supplement: Advertising, no. 31159.

Jalal al-din Mirza Qajar, *Nama-i Khusrawan: Dastan-i Padishahan-i Pars bi Zaban-i Parsi ki Sudmand Marduman bivij-i Kudakan Ast: Nakhustin Nama, az Aghaz-i Abadiyan ta Anjam-i Sasanian* (Tehran: 1285/1868).

Javadi, H., "MOLLA NASREDDIN i. THE PERSON", in *Encyclopædia Iranica*, 15 July 2009, available online: https://www.iranicaonline.org/articles/molla-nasreddin-i-the-person.

Jentink, F.A., *Verslag omtrent het Rijks-Museum van Natuurlijke Historie te Leiden, Loopende Over het Tijdvak van 1° September 1891 tot 1° September 1982* (Leiden: 1892).

Karimzada Tabrizi, M.A., *Ahwal wa Asar-i Naqqashan-i Qadim-i Iran wa Barkhi az Mashahir-i Nigar-gar-i Hind wa Osmani*, vol. 1 (London: 1363/1985).

Khalili, N.D. & Robinson, B.W. & Stanley, T., *Lacquer of the Islamic Lands Pt. 1* (London: 1993).

Khalili, N.D. & Robinson, B.W. & Stanley, T. & Bayani, M., *Lacquer of the Islamic Lands Pt. 2* (London: 1997).

Leiden University Libraries Collection Guides, *Albertus Paulus Hermanus Hotz archive and collection*, https://collectionguides.universiteitleiden.nl/resources/ublo63.

Mahdavi, Sh., "Childhood in Qajar Iran", *Iranian Studies* 47.2 (2014), 305-26.

Marzolph, U., "Molla Nasr al-Din in Persia", *Iranian Studies* 28.3/4 (1995), 157-74.

Marzolph, U. & Zenhari, R., *Mirzā ʿAli-Qoli Khoʾi: The Master Illustrator of Persian Lithographed Books in the Qajar Period*, 2 vols. (Leiden & Boston: 2022).

Masaharu Yoshida, *Safar-nama-yi Yusida Masaharu: naḵostin ferestada-yi Japon ba Iran dar dawra-yi Qajar, 1297-98 h.q.* trans. H. Rajabzadeh (Tehran: 1373/1994).

Massoudi, Sh., ""Kheimeh Shab Bazi": Iranian Traditional Marionette Theatre", *Asian Theatre Journal* 26.2 (2009), 260-80.

Mirza Tahir Munshi Isfahani, *Tazkira Ganj-i Shaygan* (Tehran: 1272/1855).

Morier, J., *The adventures of Hajji Baba of Ispahan*, ed. Ch.J. Wills (London: 1897).

Muʿayyir al-Mamalik, D., "Rijal-i ʿAsr-i Nasiri", *Yaghma* 108:4 (1336/1957), 168-75.

Muhammad Hassan Saniʿ al-Dawla Iʿtimad al-Saltana, *Tarikh-i Muntazim-i Nasiri*, I. Rizvani (ed.), 3 vols. (Tehran: 1363/1984).

Mumtahin al-Dawla, *Khatirat-i Mumtahin al-Dawla: Zindigi nama-i Mirza Mahdi Khan Mumtahin al-Dawla Shaqaqi*, H. Khanshaqaqi (ed.) (Tehran: 1362/1983).

Omidsalar, M., "ESFAND", in *Encyclopædia Iranica*, vol. VIII, Fasc. 6, 583-84, available online: https://iranicaonline.org/articles/esfand.

"Perzië op de Tentoonstelling", *Nieuwe Amsterdamsche Courant, Algemeen Handelsblad*, 01-08-1883, no. 16738.

Polak, J.E., *Persien das Land und seine Bewohner von Dr. Jacob Eduard Polak* (Leipzig: 1865).

Polak, J.E., *Description des articles exposés à l'Exposition internationale, coloniale et d'exportation générale d'Amsterdam 1883 par Perzische Handels-Vereeniging J.C.P. Hotz en Zoon, Rotterdam* (s.l.: 1883).

Porter, V. & Rosser-Owen, M. (ed.), *Metalwork and Material Culture in the Islamic World: Art, Craft and Text. Essays presented to James W. Allan* (London & New York: 2012).

Rochard, Ph., *The Zurkhāneh and Its Milieu: A Study of Traditional Athletics in Iran* (Boston, MA: 2025).

Schwerda, M.X., "Amorous Couples: Depictions of Permitted and Prohibited Love", in Roxburgh, D. (eds.), *An Album of Artists' Drawings from Qajar Iran* (Cambridge, MA: 2017), 78-83.

Sheikhi, A. & Ghafarpoor, L., Ramz-Gushai luh-i Sufali-yi Kashf Shudi az Muhavat-yi Islami-yi Shadi-yakh-i Nishapur (Decoding the Terracotta Tablet Found in Shadyakh Islamic Site of Neishabour), Fasl-nama *Negareh* 32 (1393/2015), 26-37.

Suhrabi, B., "Early Swedish Travelers to Persia, Iranian Studies", *Iranian Studies* 38.4 (2005), 631-60.

Tahvildar, Mirza Hussain Khan, *Jughrafiya-yi Isfahan*, M., Sotoudeh (ed.) (Tehran: 1342/1963).

Tawfiq Kitabkhana (ed.), *Tawfiq book: Mulla Nasruddin: the first illustrated collection of the famous jokes of 'Mulla' as the cartoon strip* (Negin: 1348/1969).

"Perzië", *Utrechtsch provinciaal en stedelijk dagblad*, 19-10-1883, no.288.

Vuurman, C., "'Greetings from Shiraz, the city of the purest air and clearest sky in the world': Ordinary Pictorial Delights from the Collections of Leiden University Library", *History of photography: The First Hundred Years of Iranian Photography* 37.1 (2013), 32-47.

Vuurman, C. & Barjesteh van Waalwijk van Doorn, F., "Vividly Painted Watercolours: Artistic Purchases from Persian Bazaars", *Qajar studies: journal of the International Qajar Studies Association* 12/13 (2013), 53-141.

Vuurman, C., *Nineteenth-century Persia in the photographs of Albert Hotz: images from the Hotz photograph collection of Leiden University Library, the Netherlands* (Rotterdam: 2011).

Vuurman, C. & Martens, Th., *Perzië en Hotz: beelden uit de fotocollectie-Hotz in de Leidse Universiteits-bibliotheek: catalogus bij een tentoonstelling in de Leidse Universiteitsbibliotheek van 30 januari tot 4 maart 1995 (Ramadan tentoonstelling 1415)* (Leiden: 1995).

Wills, Ch.J., *In the Land of the Lion and Sun; or Modern Persia. Being experiences of life in Persia from 1866 to 1881* (London: 1842).

Witkam, J.J., "Albert Hotz and his photographs of Iran: An introduction to the Leiden Collection", in Islami, K. (ed.), *Iran and Iranian Studies: Essays in Honor of Iraj Afshar* (Princeton: 1998), 276-87.

Index